Jacob's
Dozen

A Prophetic Look at
the Tribes of Israel

William C. Varner

The Friends of Israel Gospel Ministry, Inc.
Bellmawr, NJ

Jacob's Dozen: A Prophetic Look at the Tribes of Israel

William C. Varner

Copyright © 1987 by The Friends of Israel Gospel Ministry, Inc.,
Bellmawr, NJ 08099

Eighth Printing 2016

Library of Congress Catalog Card Number: 87-082384

ISBN-10 0-915540-39-8
ISBN-13 978-0-915540-39-6

Cover by Catie Perseo

Visit our website at foi.org

This book is dedicated to Mr. George W. Kern of Willow Grove, Pennsylvania. When I was a young pastor, "Bud" Kern challenged me to study the Jewish people—their history and their role in the plan of God. This book is the result of that challenge.

CONTENTS

THE TWELVE TRIBES IN BIBLICAL TIMES

○ Designated city of refuge

Mount Hermon

Tyre
Dan (Leshem)
Kedesh
Hazor
ASHER
NAPHTALI
BASHAN
Acco
EAST MANASSEH
Hannathon
Sea of Galilee
Golan
Mediterranean Sea
Helkath?
ZEBULUN
Beth-shemesh?
Dor
ISSACHAR
Edrei
Megiddo
Jezreel
Beth-shean
Ramoth-gilead
En-gannim
GILEAD
WEST MANASSEH
Zaphon?
Shechem
Mahanaim?
Jabbok River
Joppa
Tappuah
EPHRAIM
DAN
Lod
GAD
AMMON
Jabneel
Jericho
Jazer?
Rabbah
Aijalon
BENJAMIN
Beth-hoglah
Ashdod
Heshbon?
Bezer?
Ashkelon
Gath
Beth-shemesh
Jerusalem
Jordan River
Dead Sea
REUBEN
Gaza
JUDAH
Hebron
Engedi
Dibon
Sharuhen?
Beersheba
Arnon River
MOAB
SIMEON
Hormah?
NEGEB
Zered Brook
Brook of Egypt?
EDOM
Bozrah
Kadesh-barnea

0   10   20   30   40 mi
0 10 20 30 40 50 60 km

CHAPTER ONE

Jacob and His Sons

And Jacob called unto his sons, and said, Gather yourselves together, that I may tell you that which shall befall you in the last days. Gather yourselves together, and hear, ye sons of Jacob; and hearken unto Israel, your father (Gen. 49:1-2).

The old man gathered his strength and sat up on the bed with his feet on the floor. He sensed that the end was near. Looking back over a life that had its victories and defeats, Jacob could certainly testify that God had been faithful to him, even though he had not always followed God's direction. Jacob could see no future for himself, but God had revealed to him the future of his descendants in a most remarkable way. "And Jacob called unto his sons, and said, Gather yourselves together, that I may tell you that which shall befall you in the last days" (v. 1).

Jacob's 12 sons, born over a period of approximately 23 years through four different mothers, gathered reverently around the aged patriarch. What thoughts must have raced through their minds! They recalled the stories about their great-grandfather Abraham, whom God had called from Ur of the Chaldees, and who had come into the land of Canaan without even knowing his exact destination. Doubtless, they had heard times without number as they sat around the campfire about Abraham's old and barren wife, Sarah, who had miraculously given birth to a son, Isaac. They must have laughed when told that Isaac, whose name meant "laughter," was given that name because Sarah had laughed when the Lord told her she would have a son. Isaac, their grandfather, had been forbidden to marry a woman of Canaan. They must have enjoyed hearing the exciting account of Abraham's servant who was sent to find a bride for Isaac among their kinsmen in Haran and returned with the beautiful Rebekah. What thoughts now filled their minds as they looked upon their aged father, who no doubt had related to them the trials and triumphs of his own sojourn on Earth? Jacob, whose name meant "heel," had, through deceit, stolen his brother Esau's birthright and blessing, only to be exiled from the land of Canaan for more than 20 years because he was unwilling to wait for God's timing in his life.

Now they were all in Egypt—all 12 of the brothers with their families and Jacob their father. They had been reunited with their brother Joseph, whom they had sold into slavery in Egypt years before. They now understood that the hand of God had overruled their evil deed, for Joseph had eventually risen to the position of vice-regent of Egypt and was caring for their needs while famine raged in the land of Canaan.

While such memories must have flooded their minds, now was a time to look forward, not backward. *What will become of us when Jacob departs this life? Will we and our descendants stay forever in Egypt? Who will be the recipient of the birthright? Through which of us will the promised seed arrive someday?* They must have asked each other on innumerable occasions these and other questions. The moment had now arrived when they would learn the answers. "Gather yourselves together, and hear, ye sons of Jacob; and hearken unto Israel, your father" (v. 2).

Such is the background of one of the most fascinating yet neglected chapters in the Word of God. Genesis 49 provides a prophetic insight into the ancestry of the Jewish people, who today trace their history back to these 12 sons: Reuben, Simeon, Levi, Judah, Zebulun, Issachar, Dan, Gad, Asher, Naphtali, Joseph, and Benjamin. The accounts of these sons and the tribes that issued from them actually form the dramatic narrative of the remainder of the Bible. In Jewish tradition, each tribe has a symbol, and these symbols have been portrayed in synagogues, tapestries, jewelry, bookends, and countless works of art throughout the ages. One of the most famous of these works is that remarkable creation of the French Jewish artist, Marc Chagall—the beautiful windows in the synagogue of the Hadassah Medical Center in Jerusalem. But what

stories do these symbols portray? All of the symbols can be traced back
to Jacob's prophetic blessings pronounced on his sons in Genesis 49.

A remarkable fact uncovered by this writer is that, to his knowledge,
there is no full-length book in print describing the biblical history of
each of the 12 tribes. Perhaps this work will help fill that surprising void.

"All these are the twelve tribes of Israel: and this is that which their
father spoke unto them, and blessed them; every one, according to his
blessing, he blessed them" (v. 28).

Jacob's deathbed blessings on his sons recorded in Genesis 49:3–27
provide one of the most amazing examples of predictive prophecy in the
Bible. The chapter is one of many instances of prophecies given in earlier
times which clearly had their fulfillment in later biblical history. There
are two types of predictive prophecy. An unfulfilled prophecy is one
that has not yet been fulfilled in history. Some examples of unfulfilled
prophecies are the rule of the Antichrist (Dan. 7:23–27; Rev. 13:1–10),
the Second Coming of Christ (Zech. 14:3–4; Rev. 19:11–16) and the
Millennial reign of Christ (Zech. 14:9; Rev. 20:1–10). Examples of
fulfilled prophecies include the birth of the Messiah (Isa. 7:14; Mic.
5:2), His crucifixion (Ps. 22; Isa. 53), and His resurrection and ascension
(Ps. 16; 110). Genesis 49:3–27 is an example of fulfilled prophecy. As
we examine each of the prophecies regarding Jacob's sons, we will be
amazed at the prophetic accuracy of the Word of God. Furthermore,
there are vital lessons in the experiences of each tribe that teach us
the types of virtues to imitate and mistakes to avoid in our own lives.

What does it mean to bless someone? We often use this term
without understanding its meaning. Basically, to bless someone is to
bestow life and goodness on him. There are many examples recorded
in Genesis of blessings, both from God and from man. In the garden,
God blessed the animals and Adam and Eve and commanded them
to be fruitful (Gen. 1:22, 28). He blessed the seventh day (2:3), Noah
and his sons (9:1), Abraham (12:2–3), Isaac (26:12), and Jacob (28:3;
32:29). Some examples of people blessing others include Melchizedek
blessing Abraham (14:19); Rebekah's family blessing her as she left
(24:60); and Isaac blessing both Jacob and Esau (27:23, 38–40).

In Genesis 49, as is so often the case, Jacob's blessing on each son is
consistent with the character of that son. Through prophetic inspira-
tion, Jacob was permitted to see the type of character each tribe would

display. His purpose was to reveal to them "that which shall befall you in the last days" (v. 1). The phrase *the last days* appears 14 times in the Old Testament. Sometimes this phrase clearly refers to a period of time yet future to our own day. Such a passage is Isaiah 2:2, which describes the Millennial reign of King Messiah: "And it shall come to pass in the last days, that the mountain of the LORD's house shall be established in the top of the mountains, and shall be exalted above the hills; and all nations shall flow unto it." However, in some instances this phrase simply means in subsequent years. One example of this usage is found in Daniel 2:28, which states that Nebuchadnezzar's dream described that which would befall him in "the latter days."

Most of the blessings pronounced on Jacob's sons were fulfilled during the period of the judges, approximately 600-700 years after Jacob's death. The blessing on Judah began to be fulfilled in David's day and found its final fulfillment at the First Coming of Messiah. Because we have the entire Bible before us now, we can look back and see how this astounding series of prophecies has been fulfilled.

There is probably no sight more touching than that of an old man gathering his children around him to hear his final words. The last utterances of dying men can tell us much about them. Consider the final cry of Voltaire, the French skeptic: "I am abandoned by God and man!" Contrast that statement of despair with the words of John Wesley: "The best of all is that God is with us. Farewell! Farewell!" Or, consider the poignant expression of the godly confederate general, "Stonewall" Jackson, as he lay dying from wounds received at Chancellorsville: "Let us pass over the river, and rest in the shade of the trees."

How instructive it is to consider Jacob's mention of God's abundant blessings as his hour of departure approached. He charged his sons with the responsibility of burying him in the cave of Machpelah with his parents and grandparents. The writer of Hebrews reminds us, "By faith Jacob, when he was dying" (Heb. 11:21). His faith was fervent, even when his body was frail. Certainly Jacob could have looked back with regret over mistakes made, but God's grace had been so abundant to him that he only spoke of His blessings.

May each of us be granted that dying grace which prevents the bitterness that so often mars the final days of life. That grace belongs to those who have hope, not only in this life, but also in the life to come because they know the Messiah who died and rose again to give eternal life and hope to all who trust Him. The final words of the apostle Paul express that hope so clearly: "For I am now ready to be offered, and the time of my departure is at hand. I have fought a good fight, I have finished my course, I have kept the faith; henceforth there is laid up for me a crown of righteousness, which the Lord, the righteous judge, shall give me at that day; and not to me only, but unto all them also that love his appearing" (2 Tim 4:6–8).

CHAPTER TWO

Reuben

Unstable as Water

Reuben, thou art my first-born, my might, and the beginning of my strength, the excellency of dignity, and the excellency of power. Unstable as water, thou shalt not excel, because thou wentest up to thy father's bed; then defiledst thou it: he went up to my couch (Gen. 49:3-4).

Gather yourselves together, and hear, ye sons of Jacob; and harken unto Israel, your father" (Gen. 49:2). The 12 sons had dutifully assembled to hear their father's all-important final words. Perhaps they arrayed themselves in a semicircle around their aged father as he sat on the edge of his deathbed. They may have arranged themselves in the order of their births, with the eldest, Reuben, at one end and Benjamin, the youngest, at the other. They could not be condemned for greediness if each had a question running through his mind—What blessing is reserved for me and my descendants? Jacob paused to gather his thoughts, no doubt reflecting on the flood of memories associated with his sons. Then, being mysteriously guided by the Spirit of God, he spoke directly to his oldest son: "Reuben, thou art my first-born, my might, and the beginning of my strength, the excellency of dignity, and the excellency of power. Unstable as water, thou shalt not excel, because thou wentest up to thy father's bed; then defiledst thou it: he went up to my couch" (vv. 3–4).

We are not told the physical or emotional reactions of the sons as each heard his respective blessing, but most probably Reuben's emotional state plunged from an exhilarating high to a depressing low as he heard his father's words. Jacob first reminded him of his privileged position as the firstborn of his sons: "Reuben, thou art my first-born." This statement called to mind his birth, recorded in Genesis 29:31–32: "And when the LORD saw that Leah was hated, he opened her womb: but Rachel was barren. And Leah conceived, and bore a son, and she called his name Reuben; for she said, Surely the LORD hath looked upon my affliction; now therefore my husband will love me." The intrigues, jealousies, and maneuverings that existed between Jacob's wives must have been legion. In spite of the fact that Rachel eventually became Jacob's wife, she seemed to be mocked by her initial inability to bear children. And yet, Leah, her older sister (and certainly not Jacob's first choice as a wife), quickly gave birth to four sons—Reuben, Simeon, Levi, and Judah (29:32–35). When Leah saw that her firstborn was a son, she cried out, "See, a son," or *Reuben* in Hebrew.

There has always seemed to be something special, at least to a father, about a firstborn son. Although God has blessed this author with two beautiful daughters who are a delight and joy, I will never forget the special feeling when my wife delivered our firstborn child. Helen's first words were, "Honey, you have your son!" Jacob must have felt the same elation over his firstborn son. He called him "the excellency of dignity, and the excellency of power." In ancient Israel, a family's firstborn son was accorded a special privilege—a double portion of the father's inheritance (Dt. 21:17). This meant that if a father had 12 sons, he divided his inheritance into 13 parts, and the firstborn received twice the amount received by each of his brothers. Such a double inheritance was Reuben's by right of his status as firstborn son; but, alas, he did not receive that which should have been his. Furthermore, the firstborn son in ancient Israel was to be the natural leader of his brothers. Reuben, however, did not enjoy this privilege and responsibility either.

First Chronicles 5:1–3 states the reason: "Now the sons of Reuben, the first-born of Israel (for he was the first-born; but, forasmuch as he defiled his father's bed, his birthright was given unto the sons of Joseph, the son of Israel, and the genealogy is not to be reckoned after the birthright; for Judah prevailed above his brethren, and of him came the prince; but the birthright was Joseph's)." Reuben received neither the double inheritance nor the leadership role! Joseph and Judah respectively fell heir to these important blessings. But why? Genesis 49:4 reveals the shocking answer: "Unstable as water, thou shalt not excel, because thou wentest up to thy father's bed; then defiledst thou it: he went up to my couch." The words must have hit Reuben like a lightning bolt! Jacob now publicly revealed the sin which Reuben had committed, as recorded in Genesis 35:22: "And it came to pass, when Israel dwelt in that land, that Reuben went and lay with Bilhah, his father's concubine: and Israel heard it." Reuben's unbridled passion had resulted in the sin of adultery—within his own father's household! Although we are told that "Israel heard it," Jacob evidently did not confront Reuben about his transgression at that time. More than 20 years had now passed, and apparently even his brothers were not aware of the deed. This is indicated by the concluding statement of Jacob's prophecy, in which he shifted to the third person, "he [Reuben] went up to my couch." At this point, Jacob revealed to the other brothers Reuben's shameful deed.

"Unstable as water" (49:4). It was this trait that marked Reuben and would characterize his descendants. A study of the subsequent behavior of the tribe of Reuben reveals the amazing way in which this instability stamped that tribe. The most prominent persons to appear in the tribe of Reuben were two individuals named Dathan and Abiram. Due to their instability, they joined the rebellion of Korah the Levite recorded in Number 16. This group questioned the leadership of Moses and Aaron, and God's judgment upon them was swift and sure—the earth swallowed them and their entire families, thus ending the "gainsaying of Korah" (Jude 11).

Later, when the tribes were about to cross into the Promised Land, conquer it, and receive their respective portions, Reuben joined with Gad and half of Manasseh in requesting portions on the east side of the Jordan River (Num. 32). Although they reasoned that the land was better suited for their cattle, and in spite of the fact that their men did help to conquer the west side of the Jordan along with their brothers, this request revealed their instability. They were unwilling to wait for the land that God eventually would have given them, thus settling for second best. Furthermore, their action later resulted in misunderstanding and near civil war (cf. Josh. 22).

The most blatant example of Reuben's instability is recorded in the

beautiful "Song of Deborah and Barak" found in Judges 5, which mentions the tribes who "willingly offered themselves" (v. 2) in the battle
against Sisera described in the previous chapter. Such tribes as Zebulun
and Naphtali were praised for their willingness to risk their lives in battle
(v. 18). Reuben, however, was criticized for his hesitating instability:
"Why abodest thou among the sheepfolds, to hear the bleatings of the
flocks? [In] the divisions of Reuben there were great searchings of heart"
(v. 16). Reuben may have seriously considered sending troops, but his
concern to hear the "bleatings" of his own sheep overrode his patriotic
commitment. This is an illustration of so many of God's people today
who let personal concerns take precedence over their involvement in
the cause of the Lord and His work.

Jacob's prophecy foretold the insignificant future of Reuben: "Unstable as water, thou shalt not excel" (Gen. 49:4). Reuben never excelled
in his tribal development. In the census taken of the tribes at the end
of the wilderness journey, Reuben's population evidently had already
begun to decrease (cf. Num. 1:20 [46,500] with Num. 26:7 [43,730]).
By the time Moses blessed the tribes before he died, Reuben may have
been in danger of extinction, since Moses prayed, "Let Reuben live,
and not die; and let not his men be few" (Dt. 33:6).

The most significant truth about Reuben is not what is said about
him, but what is not said about him! Reuben produced not one single
prophet, military leader, judge, or important person in the history of
Israel. As a matter of fact, the most impressive contribution made by
Reuben seems to be the lending of his name to a delicious corned beef
and sauerkraut sandwich!

"Unstable as water, thou shalt not excel." Reuben lost his birthright
and leadership position because of his instability. The New Testament
states, "A double-minded man is unstable in all his ways" (Jas. 1:8).
Instability due to an inability to make proper decisions doomed Reuben
and his descendants to a future of obscurity.

Two lessons loom large from the example of Jacob's firstborn. The first
lesson is that long-range tragic effects can result from a fleeting act of
sin. Reuben's few moments of unbridled passion with Bilhah were not
worth the sorrow caused to Jacob and eventually to Reuben himself. A
wise man once said, "Don't sacrifice the permanent on the altar of the
immediate." There are men in prison and girls in shame who learned

that lesson too late and are experiencing the permanent damage that often results from an immediate gratification of lust.

The second lesson follows: Our sins can be forgiven, but the effects of our sins often must still be experienced. Jewish tradition alleges that Reuben eventually repented of his sin with Bilhah. This may have been so, since he later saved Joseph's life from the murderous plot of the other jealous brothers (Gen. 37:20–30). This was not enough, however, to remove the scar of the earlier wound, even though that wound may have healed. "But whoso committeth adultery with a woman lacketh understanding; he that doeth it destroyeth his own soul. A wound and dishonor shall he get; and his reproach shall not be wiped away" (Prov. 6:32–33).

The true story is told of a small boy who discovered his father's hammer and can of nails and proceeded to practice his carpentry. He decided to practice, however, on a freshly painted barn door. When his father discovered the deed, he determined that, in lieu of a spanking, the best discipline would be to have the boy remove each nail from the door. After struggling for a few hours, the laborious discipline was completed—and the little boy's wrist felt like butter! When the last nail was removed, he stood back, looked at the door and, instead of emitting a sigh of relief, broke out in tears and cried to his father, "Daddy, I pulled out all the nails, but the holes are still there!"

Reuben had to live with the results of his sin. May we be so on guard in moments of weakness that we are spared the emotional and physical scarring resulting from sinful deeds which, although forgiven, cause damage to ourselves and others and cannot be erased easily. God forgives and forgets—it is often much harder for us and those we may offend to do the same.

CHAPTER THREE

Simeon and Levi

Partners in Crime

Simeon and Levi are brethren; instruments of cruelty are in their habitations. O my soul, come not thou into their secret; unto their assembly, mine honor, be not thou united; for in their anger they slew a man, and in their self-will they hamstrung oxen. Cursed be their anger, for it was fierce; and their wrath, for it was cruel: I will divide them in Jacob, and scatter them in Israel (Gen. 49:5–7).

The 12 sons of the aged Jacob had arrayed themselves about his deathbed, and the patriarch had issued to Reuben his portion (i.e., because of Reuben's sin he would forfeit the double blessing of the firstborn, Gen. 49:3–4). Without hesitation, Jacob then proceeded to the next two sons—Simeon and Levi.

Simeon was the second son born to Jacob and Leah. The name Simeon (or *Shimon*) is related to the Hebrew word for "hear." Leah gave him this name because of the hope she expressed at his birth, recorded in Genesis 29:33: "And she conceived again, and bore a son; and said, Because the LORD hath heard that I was hated, he hath therefore given me this son also: and she called his name Simeon."

Levi was the third son born to Jacob and Leah. The name *Levi* means "joined" and was given to him also because of a hope expressed by Leah at his birth, recorded in Genesis 29:34: "And she conceived again, and bore a son; and said, Now this time will my husband become attached unto [be joined unto] me, because I have borne him three sons: therefore was his name called Levi."

The brothers must have grown up together, not only close in age but also in interests. Jacob began his prophecy about them by reminding them of their closeness: "Simeon and Levi are brethren" (49:5). Since all of the sons were brothers, something more must be meant by this term than just biological brothers. Simeon and Levi were also brothers in their outlook and interests. They were brothers by joining together in common actions. Perhaps a better word to describe their relationship would be partners—in this case, partners in crime.

The particular crime to which Jacob referred is recounted in Genesis 34:1–31 and can be summarized as follows: Dinah, the only daughter of Jacob and Leah and thus the sister of Simeon and Levi, was seduced by Shechem, son of Hamor, a prominent Canaanite prince. Afterward, Shechem expressed to his father a desire to have Dinah as his wife. Hamor approached Jacob with the request that he give Dinah to his son as his wife, also suggesting that the two groups consider intermarriage with one another. Simeon and Levi, however, were furious that their sister had been defiled in this manner, and they conspired to deceive Hamor and Shechem by a diabolically clever ruse. They reminded the Canaanites that they could never give their daughters to uncircumcised men. However, they continued, if the men of the city would agree to become circumcised, "Then will we give our daughters unto you, and we will take your daughters to us, and we will dwell with you, and we will become one people" (v. 16). Shechem quickly consented to what he considered a small price to pay for Dinah, whom he must have loved sincerely. He and his father also convinced the other men of their city to be circumcised, confident that this would enable them to share their respective daughters, animals, and possessions. On the third day, "when they were sore" (v. 25), the sinister nature of the plot was unveiled. Simeon and Levi, with swords in hand, suddenly came into the city and viciously slaughtered all the males, who were unable to adequately defend themselves. They plundered the city and took the wives and children captive. When Jacob learned of the vicious deed, he cried out to Simeon and Levi, "Ye have troubled me to make me odious among the inhabitants of the land, among the Canaanites and the Perizzites: and I being few in number, they shall gather themselves

together against me, and slay me; and I shall be destroyed, I and my
house" (v. 30).

Now, more than 40 years later, Jacob confronted Simeon and Levi
about their partnership in crime. He separated himself completely
from their scheme: "O my soul, come not thou into their secret [plot]"
(49:6). He also described the insidious nature of their deed. The phrase
"they hamstrung oxen" further elaborates the cruelty of the crime. Their
fierce anger and cruel wrath (v. 7) were inconsistent with their position
as the sons of Israel, "the prince with God." While every sensitive soul
can sympathize with the brothers' outrage over their sister's disgrace,
it cannot be denied that they went far beyond even vigilante justice in
the cruel vengeance they perpetrated on the men of Shechem.

What a tragic example of acting under the impulse of an uncon-
trolled rage! Many achievements for God can be destroyed through the
violent outburst of an ungoverned temper. Solomon warns us, "He that
hath no rule over his own spirit is like a city that is broken down, and
without walls" (Prov. 25:28). In his excellent book, *The History of Joseph*,
George Lawson writes, "In the heat of passion a man is not his own
master, he is the slave of an infernal lust. He is worse than a madman,
because he has no more command of himself than a madman, and what
understanding is left to him only serves to fit him for doing the greater
mischief."[1] How desperately we need that character trait called tem-
perance, or self–control, which is a "fruit of the Spirit" (Gal. 5:22-23).

Because of their misdeeds, Jacob pronounced the following prophecy
on the descendants of Simeon and Levi: "I will divide them in Jacob,
and scatter them in Israel" (Gen. 49:7). The meaning is simple: neither
Simeon nor Levi would possess his own separate portion of the Promised Land. When the tribes settled in the land, each would be allotted
a separate inheritance. Simeon and Levi, however, would be scattered
throughout the tribal portions.

The way in which this was fulfilled in the history of the tribes of
Simeon and Levi is a remarkable evidence of the accuracy of Bible
prophecy. Joshua chapters 1—12 describe the initial conquest of the
land of Canaan by the Israelite forces, and chapters 13—21 record the
division of the land among the victorious tribes. Special allocations,
however, were made for the tribes of Simeon and Levi. Simeon's
portion is described in Joshua 19:1-9. "And the second lot came forth

to Simeon, even for the tribe of the children of Simeon according to their families; and their inheritance was within the inheritance of the children of Judah" (v. 1). Seventeen cities and their surrounding villages are then mentioned that would belong to Simeon (vv. 2–8). Finally, we read, "Out of the portion of the children of Judah was the inheritance of the children of Simeon; for the portion of the children of Judah was too much for them. Therefore the children of Simeon had their inheritance within the inheritance of them" (v. 9). Judah's portion was the southernmost of all the tribes and stretched from the Mediterranean Sea on the west to the Dead Sea on the east, and from below Jerusalem on the north to below Beersheba in the south. The cities within Judah that were assigned to Simeon were all in the arid and barren region known as the Negev—a most inhospitable area for cultivation and the settled life. This divided existence, without a centralized tribal organization, was an apt fulfillment of Jacob's words, "I will divide them in Jacob, and scatter them in Israel" (49:7)!

Tracing the history of the tribe of Simeon is easy, since there are very few references to the tribe following the conquest. It is interesting to note how the tribe decreased in number from the beginning to the end of the wilderness wandering. In Numbers 1:23 their adult male population is recorded as 59,300, while in Numbers 26:14 (nearly 40 years later) it is 22,200. Leon Wood in *A Survey of Israel's History* suggests that this great reduction was due to the men of Simeon being deeply involved in the idolatry of Baal-peor recorded in Numbers 25:1–18.[2] The only individual Israelite mentioned in that sin was a Simeonite (Zimri, v. 14). Also, a plague killed 24,000 Israelites, probably many of them from the tribe of Simeon (v. 9).

It is difficult to know exactly what happened to Simeon when the united kingdom was divided into northern and southern kingdoms during the reign of Rehoboam, son of Solomon. Certain Israelites who were faithful to the Lord God migrated into Judah at that time (2 Chr. 11:16), some of whom were Simeonites. During the reign of Hezekiah, a large group of Simeonites migrated farther south to the land of Edom, where they conquered and displaced the Amalekites who dwelt there (1 Chr. 4:38–43). Certain later references suggest the possibility that many Simeonites had also migrated to the northern kingdom, for they are mentioned in conjunction with the tribes of Ephraim and Manasseh

(2 Chr. 15:9; 34:6). Regardless of the outcome of the tribe, their small number and few references are testimony to the truth of Jacob's prophecy, "I will divide them in Jacob, and scatter them in Israel."

Jewish interpreters have taken notice of the history of Simeon. In Jewish tradition, all poor Jews supposedly came from that ill-fated tribe.

The way in which Jacob's prophecy of scattering was fulfilled among the descendants of Levi is even more fascinating. In Numbers 35:1–4, the Lord commanded that the Levites be given cities instead of a portion of the land. Joshua 21:1–42 records that the Levites were given a total of 48 cities with their suburbs. These cities were scattered throughout the territories of the other tribes. Thus, Jacob's prophecy, "I will divide them in Jacob, and scatter them in Israel," was literally fulfilled. Although landless regarding their inheritance, the Levites actually were the most privileged of all the tribes, for Deuteronomy 10:9 states, "Wherefore Levi hath no part nor inheritance with his brethren; the LORD is his inheritance, according as the LORD thy God promised him." The Levites were given the honored position of representing the other tribes before the Lord and the right to bear the Ark of the Covenant and care for the holy articles of the Tabernacle. From the family of Aaron, within the tribe of Levi, came the priests who were privileged to offer the sacrifices of the people. Both priests and Levites were financially supported by the tithes of the people, thus enabling them to give their full time to ministering before the Lord (18:1-5).

Deuteronomy 33 records the blessings of Moses on the tribes before his death. It is striking to note that, whereas Simeon is the only tribe omitted from his blessings, the longest blessing is given to Levi (vv. 8–11). Consider some of what Moses says of the Levites, "Let thy Thummim and thy Urim be with thy holy one . . . They shall teach Jacob thine ordinances, and Israel thy law" (vv. 8, 10).

How is it that the prohecy which proved to be a curse for the Simeonites actually turned into a blessing for the Levites? The answer is found in Exodus 32, which records the awful sin of the Israelites in worshiping a golden calf. This sin was compounded by the fact that it was encouraged by Aaron while his brother Moses was on the mountain receiving the Law from the Lord! When Moses came down from the mountain and saw the shameful sight, he shattered the tablets of stone in righteous anger. After personally destroying the calf, he decided that radical spiritual surgery had to be performed on the people. The biblical text itself says it best:

And when Moses saw that the people were naked (for Aaron had made them naked unto their shame among their enemies), then Moses stood in the gate of the camp, and said, Who is on the LORD's side? Let him come unto me. And all the sons of Levi gathered themselves together unto him. And he said unto them, Thus saith the LORD God of Israel, Put every man his sword by his side, and go in and out from gate to gate throughout the camp, and slay every man his brother, and every man his companion, and every man his neighbor. And the children of Levi did according to the word of Moses: and there fell of the people that day about three thousand men. For Moses had said, Consecrate yourselves today to the LORD, even every man upon his son, and upon his brother, that he may bestow upon you a blessing this day (vv. 25–29).

Earlier, the zeal of Levi had resulted in the death of the Shechemites—a deed deplored by Jacob. In this instance, however, through their obedience to Moses, the Levites demonstrated their zeal in a righteous cause. For this zeal, they were awarded the special place they have enjoyed throughout Jewish history. While later reflecting upon this incident, Moses reminded the people, "At that time the LORD set apart the tribe of Levi, to bear the ark of the covenant of the LORD, to stand before the LORD to minister unto him, and to bless in his name, unto this day" (Dt. 10:8). The final prophet of the Old Covenant reminds us, "And ye shall know that I have sent this commandment unto you, that my covenant might be with Levi, saith the LORD of hosts. My covenant was with him of life and peace; and I gave them to him for the fear with which he feared me, and was afraid before my name" (Mal. 2:4–5).

Even though today there is no Tabernacle, Temple, sacrifice or functioning priesthood, the Levites and priests still have certain privileges and responsibilities. Documents that prove Jewish tribal lineages perished in the destruction of Jerusalem in AD 70, so Jews can no longer prove their tribal origins. There is, however, an unbroken oral tradition regarding the identity of the descendants of the Levites and the priests within the tribe of Levi.

Those priests (*cohanim*) and Levites have certain privileges in the synagogue ritual, such as being the first to be called upon to read the Torah and the ones who bless the congregation at the end of the service (cf. Num. 6:23–26). Thus, even today Levi continues to be set apart from the rest of Israel. Certainly Simeon and Levi were zealous, but their zeal was not channeled into godly paths. Zeal in itself is not sufficient, even in the Lord's work. There are those who think that activity, devotion, commitment, and sincerity are the only necessities in serving the Lord. Such zeal, however, can be misdirected. We must remember Paul's earnest remark about his Jewish kinsmen according to the flesh, "Brethren, my heart's desire and prayer to God for Israel is, that they might be saved. For I bear them witness that they have a zeal for God, but not according to knowledge" (Rom. 10:1–2). Paul had firsthand knowledge of a zeal for God that was counter productive, as expressed in Philippians 3:4–6: "Though I might also have confidence in the flesh. If any other man thinketh that he hath reasons for which he might trust in the flesh, I more: circumcised the eighth day, of the stock of Israel, of the tribe of Benjamin, an Hebrew of the Hebrews; as touching the law, a Pharisee; concerning zeal, persecuting the church; touching the righteousness which is in the law, blameless." Just as Levi redirected his zeal into godly channels, Paul redirected his zeal into service for the Messiah, whom he had once so inexorably opposed.

May the lessons of Simeon, Levi, and Paul teach us to focus our zeal on God's program and purposes, not on our own selfish plans.

CHAPTER FOUR

Judah

Tribe of King Messiah

Judah, thou art he whom thy brethren shall praise: thy hand shall be in the neck of thine enemies; thy father's children shall bow down before thee. Judah is a lion's whelp: from the prey, my son, thou art gone up: he stooped down, he crouched as a lion, and as an old lion. Who shall rouse him up? The scepter shall not depart from Judah, nor a lawgiver from between his feet, until Shiloh come; and unto him shall the gathering of the people be (Gen. 49:8–10).

If a poll were taken to determine which of Jacob's 12 sons were the most famous, certainly either Joseph or Judah would be the favored one. Although more space in the Scriptures is given to the personal history of Joseph than any of his brothers (Gen. 37—50), far more is said about the tribe of Judah than any other tribe.

Reuben, through his unstable act of immorality, had forfeited both the double portion of his father's inheritance and his position as firstborn among his brothers (49:3–4). That Joseph and Judah were the benefactors of this forfeiture is clearly stated in 1 Chronicles 5:1–2. Reuben's right to the double inheritance was forfeited to Joseph, and his right to the position of leadership over his brothers was forfeited to Judah.

The two longest patriarchal blessings in Genesis 49 are reserved for Judah and Joseph. Judah's blessing is recorded in Genesis 49:8–12. It follows the prophecies on his three older brothers, Reuben, Simeon, and Levi, each of whom had committed questionable acts affecting Jacob's commentaries regarding them. In contrast to those prophecies of doom is the series of prophetic blessings pronounced upon Judah and his descendants.

> *Judah, thou art he whom thy brethren shall praise: thy hand shall be in the neck of thine enemies; thy father's children shall bow down before thee. Judah is a lion's whelp: from the prey, my son, thou art gone up: he stooped down, he crouched as a lion, and as an old lion. Who shall rouse him up? The scepter shall not depart from Judah, nor a lawgiver from between his feet, until Shiloh come; and unto him shall the gathering of the people be* (vv. 8–10).

Four prophecies about Judah appear in these verses.

JUDAH WILL BE THE LEADER OF HIS BROTHERS

"Judah, thou art he whom thy brethern shall praise: . . . thy father's children shall bow down before thee" (v. 8). In this amazing series of blessings, Jacob often employed a play on words. It is appropriate that Judah would be praised by his brothers since his name means "praise." The account of his birth makes this clear: "And she [Leah] conceived again, and bore a son: and she said, Now will I praise the LORD: therefore she called his name Judah; and ceased bearing" (29:35). Thus, Judah, whose name means praise, will be praised by his brothers who will recognize his position of leadership.

Judah seemed to assume this leadership role during his lifetime. In Genesis 37:26–27, we are told that he helped to spare Joseph's life by suggesting that the brothers sell him to the Ishmaelites rather than kill him. When the brothers later went down into Egypt and were unknowingly cared for by their brother Joseph, Judah was the spokesman for the group (44:14–34).

In subsequent years, as the tribes were marching through the wilderness, it was the tribe of Judah that went first (Num. 10:14). After the Israelites conquered the land of Canaan and began to possess it, "the lot of the tribe of the children of Judah" was received first (Josh. 15:1). The tribe of Judah possessed one of the largest and most important sections in the southern part of the land of Canaan. Numbers chapters

1 and 26 list two censuses taken of the tribes of Israel at the beginning and the end of the 40-year wanderings. In both censuses, Judah had the largest tribal population.

A Jewish commentator provides an interesting insight into the leadership position of Judah. He states that today whenever a son of Jacob is asked, "Who are you?" he does not say, "I am a Reubenite or a Josephite," but he says, "I am a Judahite," or, in other words, a Jew. The name *Jew* is really a shortened form of *Judah* and came into existence after the return of the Jews from the Babylonian Captivity. Although there were representatives of all the tribes in the land at that time, Judah was the dominant tribe; hence, the land was called Judea. The people, therefore, were *Judeans* or, in a shortened form, Jews. In the New Testament, the words *Hebrew, Israelite,* and *Jew* are synonymous terms to describe the people of Israel. The apostle Paul applies all three terms to himself at various times (Acts 22:3; Rom. 11:1; Phil. 3:5). Thus, Jacob's prophecy that Judah would be the leader of his brothers was literally fulfilled.

JUDAH WILL BE A GREAT CONQUEROR

Jacob said of Judah, "Thy hand shall be in the neck of thine enemies" (Gen. 49:8). This is a graphic reference to the humiliation of one's enemies in battle. To expose the neck of one's enemy was a symbolic act signifying that the enemy had been conquered (Josh. 10:24).

The greatest conqueror in the history of Israel was King David. Second Samuel 8 records that David extended the boundaries of Israel when he subdued the Philistines, the Moabites, the Ammonites and the Edomites. David himself composed a beautiful song, recorded in both 2 Samuel 22 and Psalm 18, in which he praised God for giving him strength, particularly in battle. It is interesting that he used the very phrase employed by Jacob in his prophecy, "Thou hast also given me the necks of mine enemies, that I might destroy them who hate me"(2 Sam. 22:41 and Ps. 18:40). David was a member of the tribe of Judah. Under David's son Solomon, the boundaries of the kingdom were extended to their greatest limits as he consolidated his father's conquests (1 Ki. 4:20–25).

In this regard, Judah is compared to a lion. "Judah is a lion's whelp: from the prey, my son, thou art gone up: he stooped down, he crouched as a lion, and as an old lion. Who shall rouse him up?" (Gen. 49:9).

It is interesting to note that five different animals are associated with various tribes in Jacob's blessings. In addition to comparing Judah with a lion, Issachar is associated with a donkey (v. 14), Dan with a serpent (v. 17), Naphtali with a deer (v. 21), and Benjamin with a wolf (v. 27). In Numbers 2, the arrangement of the tribes around the camp is described. It is stated there that each tribe had a standard outside the camp to identify the tribe. Although, unfortunately, the symbols for the various tribal standards are not identified, it is probable that a lion was pictured on Judah's standard. The lion of Judah is a very prominent symbol in Jewish tradition, as borne out by its depiction on ancient coins unearthed in the Holy Land, as well as on a modern Israeli coin.

The kingly character of Judah, as mentioned in verse 10, is appropriately symbolized by the Lion who is often called the king of beasts. This theme is carried through the Scriptures, even into the New Testament. Revelation 5:5 describes a scene in the throne room of heaven in which the Lion of the tribe of Judah is the main character. This is a Messianic reference to the Lord Jesus Christ who, by descent, was a member of this tribe.

JUDAH WILL PRODUCE A ROYAL LINE OF KINGS

"The scepter shall not depart from Judah, nor a lawgiver from between his feet, until Shiloh come; and unto him shall the gathering of the people be" (Gen. 49:10). Although the early government of Israel was a theocracy rather than a monarchy, the Lord anticipated that there one day would be kings in Israel (Dt. 17:14–20). In later years, the first king of Israel, Saul, was from the tribe of Benjamin (1 Sam. 9:1–2). However, God rejected Saul and sent His prophet Samuel to anoint His choice for king: young David, in the town of Bethlehem, of the tribe of Judah (1 Sam. 16:1–13). All the legitimate kings of Israel throughout its history were descendants of David. Jacob's prophecy stated that the symbols of royalty, the scepter and the ruler's staff ("lawgiver" in the Authorized Version), would never depart from Judah. This teaches that the right to reign as king will always be with the tribe of Judah. No legitimate king could arise from another tribe.

The succession of 20 kings in the northern kingdom, beginning with Jeroboam in 930 BC and ending with Hoshea in 721 BC, were illegitimate and rejected by God. Even though some of Judah's kings were wicked, they were still in the royal line of succession. This prophecy does not mean that a king will always be reigning in Judah; however, the right of kingship will always be in this tribe and in no other.

Verse 10 further states that the scepter will not depart "until Shiloh come." Many have interpreted this phrase to mean that when Shiloh comes, the scepter will depart. This, however, is not what the verse is teaching. No mention is made of a time when the scepter will depart from Judah. The word *until* in the phrase *until Shiloh come* does not imply termination. The same word is used in God's promise to Jacob recorded in Genesis 28:15: "And, behold, I am with thee, and will keep thee in all places to which thou goest, and will bring thee again into this land; for I will not leave thee, until I have done that which I have spoken to thee of." God's assurance that He would not leave Jacob until He fulfilled the promise does not mean that He left him when the promise was fulfilled. In reality, the scepter has never departed from Judah. The promise given in Genesis 49:10 is not that the scepter will depart from Judah, but that in Shiloh the scepter will reach its greatest glory and extent.

This brings us to a consideration of the last promise given to Judah.

JUDAH WILL PRODUCE THE MESSIAH

Genesis 49:10 promises that one day "Shiloh" will come, as a result of which there is an additional prophecy: "And unto him shall the gathering of the people be." Who, or what, is meant by the term *Shiloh*? Of the many attempts which have been made to interpret the meaning of this word, let us consider the three main approaches to Shiloh mentioned in most of the commentaries.

Since Shiloh is also the name of a town in Israel, there are some who believe it is that town which is referred to in this verse. The most recent Jewish translation of the Scriptures entitled *The Tanakh* states that a literal translation of this verse is "until he comes to Shiloh." The town of Shiloh was the place where the Israelites set up the Tabernacle after the conquest (Josh. 18:1). It was the center of Israelite worship until the days of Samuel (1 Sam. 1:3). However, to render Shiloh in Genesis 49:10 as referring to this town simply results in confusion. This interpretation is a reflection of the desire to prevent this verse from referring to the Messiah. It has no basis in the text itself.

The second school of thought interprets the meaning of *Shiloh* as "to whom it belongs" and presents a reference to the Messiah to whom the scepter belongs. Often, the parallel passage of Ezekiel 21:27 is cited as support of this view: "I will overturn, overturn, overturn it, and it shall be no more, until he comes whose right it is; and I will give it him." The ancient Greek translation called the *Septuagint* interpreted Shiloh in this way. However, to translate Shiloh as "to whom it belongs" requires a change of one letter in the consonantal text of the Hebrew word. When interpreters begin to alter the text of Scripture to favor their interpretation, they are on dangerous ground. Although this interpretation does see the verse as referring to the Messiah, it cannot be accepted for this reason.

The best interpretation views Shiloh as a personal name of the Messiah (i.e., the right of kingship will always be with Judah until the Messiah comes). To Him (that is, the Messiah) the nations will submit. The Talmud lists "Shiloh" as one of the names of Messiah (Sanhedrin 98b). The most ancient Jewish commentary on the book of Genesis also adopts this interpretation (Bereshit Rabba 99). This is the view of the Authorized Version and of many evangelical commentators. The name Shiloh easily could be related to the word *Shalom*, the Hebrew word for "peace." This would agree with the prophecy of the Messiah's coming in Isaiah 9:6: "For unto us a child is born, unto us a son is given, and the government shall be upon his shoulder; and his name shall be called Wonderful, Counselor, The Mighty God, The Everlasting Father, The Prince of Peace," as well as Micah 5:5, "And this man shall be the peace." This interpretation is preferred above the others.

Undoubtedly, the meaning of the word Shiloh refers to the King Messiah—an interpretation affirmed even by the great Jewish commentator Rashi. This prophecy is one more stroke in the developing portrait of the Messiah in the Old Testament Scriptures. From that time on, people looked for the Promised One to come from the tribe of Judah. In Genesis 3:15 we are told simply that the deliverer will come from mankind (the seed of the woman). In Genesis 9:26, another characteristic is mentioned: He will be a descendant of Shem, one of the three sons of Noah. Years later, God again delineated His genealogy by saying that among the descendants of Shem, Abraham would be the progenitor of Him in whom all families of the earth would be blessed (v. 12:3). That Messianic line was further narrowed to one of the two sons of Abraham, namely Isaac (21:12). The Messianic line was again narrowed to one of the two sons of Isaac, namely Jacob (25:23). Of Jacob's 12 sons, Judah is chosen as the one through whom Messiah will come (49:10). Later in Israel's history, God chose a descendant of Judah, David, to be the family through whom the Messiah would come (2 Sam. 7:12–16). Then the genealogy was narrowed once more when a specific town within Judah, Bethlehem, was chosen as the site of Messiah's birth (Mic. 5:2).

This is but a brief outline of the Messianic credentials.

Anyone claiming to be the Messiah must present these credentials to Israel. Jesus possessed these credentials. In Matthew 1:1–16 the genealogy of Jesus is listed and clearly shows Him as one who genealogically qualifies to be the Messiah. The marvelous account in Matthew 2:1–10 of the birth of Jesus in Bethlehem was in accordance with Micah 5:2. Jesus presented these and many more credentials to Israel as their Messiah.

But someone may ask, Could a Jewish person appear in the future who would have these same credentials and be Israel's Messiah? No, he could not, because there are no records available to substantiate such a claim. When the Romans destroyed Jerusalem in AD 70, the Temple, with all of its treasures and archives, was completely destroyed as well. One of the treasures of the Temple was the records necessary to validate the family and tribal genealogies. Since that fateful day, no Jewish person has been able to prove by records his or her genealogy.

If Jesus is not the fulfillment of the "Shiloh" passage in Genesis 49:10, the awful fact facing Israel is that there never will be anyone who can prove that he fulfills the prophecies of Messiah's royal lineage. But there is One who meets all of these qualifications—the Lion of Judah, who is also the Lamb slain to redeem Jews and Gentiles from sin's bondage (see Rev. 5:5–10).

CHAPTER FIVE

Zebulun and Issachar

Merchant and Servant

Zebulun shall dwell at the haven of the sea; and he shall be for an haven of ships, and his border shall be unto Sidon (Gen. 49:13).

The aged patriarch, Jacob, continued his series of prophetic blessings on his 12 sons with brief but significant statements about Zebulun, Leah's sixthborn, and Issachar, her fifthborn.

The birth of Zebulun is recorded in Genesis 30:19–20. At that time his mother Leah expressed the hope, "now will my husband dwell with me." *Zebulun* means "dwelling." Nothing of significance about the man Zebulun is recorded in Genesis. Evidently he joined with his brethren in their common actions, such as the selling of Joseph into Egypt and their later trips to Egypt during the famine.

Jacob's prophecy about Zebulun's descendants speaks of maritime traders. They will live near the "seas" (plural in Hebrew), a reference to their tribal allotment between the Mediterranean Sea and the Sea of Galilee (see Josh. 19:10–16 and map). Located in the western end of the Valley of Jezreel, the tribe of Zebulun was traversed by one of the great trading routes of antiquity, the *Via Maris* (way of the sea). This caravan route reached from Damascus in the northeast to Egypt in the southwest. Thus, lying between two seas and on a trade route, Zebulun was heavily involved in commercial ventures. Moses' later blessing on the tribes in Deuteronomy 33 reflects this characteristic. Among other things, he says, "for they [Zebulun] shall suck the abundance of the seas, and treasures hidden in the sand" (Dt. 33: 19).

The second truth in Jacob's prophecy about Zebulun is the statement, "and his border shall be unto Sidon." Sidon (or Zidon) was a great northern Canaanite city in the land later called Phoenicia and which today is the country of Lebanon. According to the tribal allotments, Zebulun's territory was separated from Sidon by the tribe of Asher (Josh. 19:24–31). Asher, however, was never able to dislodge the Canaanites who dwelt in that coastal area north of Mount Carmel and Haifa Bay. Evidently, according to this prophecy, Zebulunites in later days began to filter into this coastal area bordering Phoenicia, thus fulfilling the prophecy. An interesting modern confirmation of this prophecy is the valley paralleling this northern coast which is called the Valley of Zebulun, although it is located in the area allotted to Asher but not conquered by that tribe.

The later history of Zebulun does not reveal any notable individuals. The most famous Zebulunite in Scripture was Elon, who judged Israel for 10 years (Jud. 12:11–12). That which is recorded about the tribe as a whole, however, is quite notable. Zebulun is memorialized in the "Song of Deborah and Barak" recorded in Judges 5. This song was composed to memorialize God's deliverance of the Israelites from the army of Jabin, king of Hazer, whose commanding officer was Sisera. The battle, recorded in Judges 4, took place in the Valley of Jezreel—in Zebulun's territory! Evidently, each tribe had the opportunity to send a contingent of volunteers to the conflict. The tribes of Reuben, Gilead (Gad), Dan, and Asher failed to respond to the call and were censured in the song (Jud. 5:15–17). Ephraim, Benjamin, Machir (Manasseh), Zebulun, Issachar, and Naphtali were commended for their willingness to volunteer for the battle (Jud. 5:14–15, 18). Particular honor was accorded to Zebulun: "Zebulun and Naphtali were a people who jeoparded their lives unto the death in the high places of the field" (Jud. 5:18). This testimony of the Zebulunites' bravery and willingness to risk their own lives for God's cause serves as a stirring example to today's soldiers for Christ. A New Testament parallel is found in that noble word of commendation for Paul and Barnabas issued by the Jerusalem church: "Men that have hazarded their lives for the name of our Lord Jesus Christ" (Acts 15:26). The trail of those saints willing to sacrifice their lives for the Lord reaches from notables of the early church, such as Stephen and Justin Martyr, through such modern martyrs as the Auca missionaries and others who suffered the ultimate human sacrifice because of their willingness to lay down their lives for the gospel.

Perhaps the characteristic that enabled Zebulun to be so bold is found in an obscure verse in that little-known but enlightening pair of books called the Chronicles: "Of Zebulun, such as went forth to battle, expert in war, with all instruments of war, fifty thousand who could keep rank; they were not of double heart" (1 Chr. 12:33). Singleness of heart and mind enabled Zebulun to be stable and successful. They kept rank and did not flee the battle because their attitude was the same as that of the apostle Paul: "But this one thing I do" (Phil. 3:13). A divided heart and mind produce instability: "A double-minded man is unstable in all his ways" (Jas. 1:8). This is the great lesson from Zebulun: courage to face the conflict due to an unswerving commitment to the goal.

Issachar is a strong ass crouching down between two burdens; and he saw that rest was good, and the land that it was pleasant; and bowed his shoulder to bear, and became a servant unto forced labor (Gen. 49:14–15).

Jacob closed his series of prophetic blessings on his sons through Leah by comparing her fifthborn son, Issachar, to a burden-bearing donkey. *Issachar* means "hire" or "wages," and he was given this name because of his mother's exclamation at his birth: "And God hearkened unto Leah, and she conceived, and bore Jacob the fifth son. And Leah said, God hath given me my hire, because I have given my maiden to my husband: and she called his name Issachar" (30:17–18). Nothing specific is known of the man Issachar. Because of this lack of information, the ancient rabbis developed traditions about him, along with the other brothers. In Jewish tradition, therefore, Issachar was a student of the Torah, while his younger brother Zebulun toiled as a merchant to support Issachar in his studies. Although there is no scriptural foundation for this tradition, the rabbis based it on Moses' blessing in Deuteronomy 33:18: "And of Zebulun he said, Rejoice, Zebulun, in thy going out [i.e., trading]; and, Issachar, in thy tents [i.e., studying]."

"Issachar is a strong ass crouching down between two burdens" (Gen.

49:14). In 20th century terminology, to call someone a donkey would not be a compliment (unless he were a Democrat!). However, no criticism was implied in Jacob's statement. Donkeys in ancient Israel were most valuable animals of service. Since it was an age without trucks and trains, donkeys carried most of the cargo that was transported (cf. Dt. 5:14; 22:10; 2 Sam. 19:26). It should be noted that the donkey was later associated with the Messiah (Zech. 9:9). An additional characteristic of Issachar is that he would be a "strong ass crouching down between two burdens." The word *burden* can also be understood as "saddle bags," the picture being a graphic one of the large saddlebags placed on each side of a crouching donkey.

There is also a geographical characteristic of Issachar portrayed in this vivid word picture. An examination of the tribal allotment to Issachar given in Joshua 19:17–22 reveals that he was assigned the fertile eastern end of the Jezreel Valley. His boundary on the north was Mount Tabor and on the south Mount Gilboa. Thus, these two mountains served as the large "burdens" on the sides of Issachar.

Jacob's final statement about his son has been misunderstood by many commentators. "And he saw that rest was good, and the land that it was pleasant; and bowed his shoulder to bear, and became a servant unto forced labor" (Gen. 49:15). One modern writer has said, "It is apparent that this pronouncement is caustic rather than complimentary"[1] (Speiser). This interpretation views the tribe as slothful and cowardly men who were content to enjoy their land without fighting to maintain its independence. This trait, however, is not characteristic of the few Issacharites mentioned in Scripture. According to Judges 10:1–2, Tola, a man of Issacher, judged Israel for 23 years and evidently was a brave leader. The references to the tribe as a whole are few but all commendatory. The great commentator Adam Clarke has summarized these references well.

The cowardice that is attributed to this tribe, certainly does not agree with the view in which they are exhibited in Scripture. In Judges 5:15 they are praised for their powerful assistance. In 1 Chronicles 7:1–5 they are said to have been "valiant men of might in all their families, and in all their generations." It appears that they were a laborious, hardy, valiant tribe, patient in labor, and invincible in war, bearing both these burdens with great constancy whenever it was necessary.[2]

The only other reference to Issachar is also complimentary: "men who had understanding of the times, to know what Israel ought to do" (1 Chr. 12:32). The men of Issachar were not only knowledgeable of God's Word, they were knowledgeable of God's world. They understood the trends of the age so that they knew how to apply God's Word to life. They did not have their heads in the sand. Jesus condemned some Pharisees and Sadducees for their lack of such insight into their age: "O ye hypocrites, ye can discern the face of the sky; but can ye not discern the signs of the times?" (Mt. 16:3). Rather than criticizing Issachar, as some commentators are prone to do, Jacob portrayed him as having insight and as one who carried the burdens of others. These traits are sorely lacking and desperately needed in God's people today. The apostle reminds us, "Bear ye one another's burdens, and so fulfill the law of Christ" (Gal. 6:2). Dear reader, are you a burden creator for others or a burden bearer? Do you help to shoulder the heavy burdens under which some of God's children labor, or do you add additional burdens to already weary shoulders? God grant us a host of Zebuluns and Issachars in our midst—men and women who are committed to the work and who care for the workers!

CHAPTER SIX

Dan

The Judge and the Serpent

Dan shall judge his people, as one of the tribes of Israel. Dan shall be a serpent by the way, an adder in the path, that biteth the horse heels, so that his rider shall fall backward. I have waited for thy salvation, O LORD (Gen. 49:16–18).

When Jacob foretold that Issachar, among other things, would be "a strong ass crouching down between two burdens" (49:14–15), he concluded his series of prophetic blessings on the six sons of his wife Leah (see vv. 1–15). The aged patriarch then turned to the four sons born to him by the two handmaids, Bilhah and Zilpah.

Bilhah was Rachel's maid whom she "gave" to Jacob because of her own inability to conceive (30:1–4). When a son was born to Bilhah, Rachel exclaimed, "God hath judged me, and hath also heard my voice, and hath given me a son: therefore called she his name Dan" (vv. 5–6). Since modern readers often question this strange procedure, it should be noted that such an action was entirely in accordance with the social customs of the day. Jacob's grandmother, Sarah, had performed a similar deed when she gave her handmaid Hagar to Abraham because she had been unable to bear children (16:1–3). Archaeology has shed light on this custom. A regulation in the famous Code of Hammurabi, an ancient legal system prevalent in the Middle East during Abraham's time, provided for just such an eventuality. This action was not commanded by God, but He did permit it as a social custom and regulated it as He did the practice of divorce (cf. Dt. 24:1–4).

Most probably Dan, along with Gad, Asher, and Naphtali (the other sons by the handmaids), grew up feeling some what inferior since they were not the sons of Jacob's wives, Leah and Rachel. Perhaps this is the reason Jacob said, "Dan shall judge his people, as one of the tribes of Israel" (Gen. 49: 16). He wanted to assure these four sons that, regardless of their so-called inferior births, they also would be included and blessed as tribal groups.

Jacob's statements about Dan and his descendants involve a famous person, a familiar problem, and, finally, a fervent prayer.

A FAMOUS PERSON

The name *Dan* means "judgment" (see Gen. 30:6). Jacob's prophecy, therefore, involves a play on words, "Dan shall judge." The Hebrew expression is *dan yadin*. The last word is the same as the name of the late Israeli archaeologist, Yigael Yadin.

Most interpreters of this passage have seen a graphic fulfillment of this prophecy in Dan's greatest son, the famous strong man-judge Samson. Judges 13:2 informs us that Samson's father Manoah was "of Zorah, of the family of the Danites." The allotment of the tribe of Dan was along the southwest Mediterranean coast of the Promised Land (see map and Josh. 19:40–48). The difficult problem for the Danites was that their land was bordered by the Philistines, Israel's ancient enemy. The Danite farms and villages were constantly oppressed by this powerful people who resented a foreign presence so near to their own centers of life. Therefore, God raised up a deliverer who would "judge" or avenge his own people on the Philistines. The exploits of Samson recorded in Judges 13—16 are famous examples of nontraditional warfare demonstrating the success of the few against the many and the small against the large. Jacob's words in verse 17 graphically described Samson's tactics: "Dan shall be a serpent by the way, an adder in the path, that biteth the horse heels, so that his rider shall fall backward." This language suggests that the principal aspects of Dan's conquests would be accomplished by cunning rather than by military confrontation. Matthew Henry has graphically described Samson's final heroic deed in this way: "When he pulled the house down under the Philistines that were upon its roof (Jud. 16:29–30), he made the horse throw his rider." Samson's defeats of the Philistines were short-lived, however. This pagan enemy continued to oppress the Danites as well as the other tribes. Jacob's prophecy, therefore, was not exhausted in Samson.

Jacob also spoke of a sad problem that would characterize the tribe of Dan.

A FAMILIAR PROBLEM

Jacob's association of a "serpent" with the tribe of Dan (Gen. 49:17) was not without significance. This was not the first mention of a serpent in Genesis. One recalls the actions of the serpent regarding the fall of Adam and Eve in Genesis 3. Throughout the Scriptures this animal is a symbol of Satan. Jesus accused His Pharisaic opponents of being spiritual descendants of this serpent: "Ye are of your father the devil, and the lusts of your father ye will do. He was a murderer from the beginning, and abode not in the truth, because there is no truth in him. When he speaketh a lie, he speaketh of his own; for he is a liar, and the father of it" (Jn. 8:44). The clearest words on this subject are found in Revelation 12:9: "And the great dragon was cast out, that old serpent, called the Devil and Satan, who deceiveth the whole world; he was cast out into the earth, and his angels were cast out with him." For this reason, Jacob's prophecy indicated that satanic influence would be dominant in Dan's future. Does the scriptural history of this tribe reveal such a satanic influence? A brief survey of references to Dan indicates that the problem of idolatry was a characteristic malady of that tribe.

The chaotic period of the judges was a time when "every man did that which was right in his own eyes' (Jud. 17:6; 21:25). No greater illustration of this moral and spiritual anarchy can be found than the sad account of the migration of the Danites recorded in Judges 18. Evidently the men of Dan had grown weary of defending their little stretch of shore from the maraudings of the Philistines. Therefore, they sent a party of five military scouts to search out other parts of the Promised Land for a better location. The scouts traveled far north to the foot of Mount Hermon, near the border of modern-day Lebanon, and found a sleepy little town called Laish (18:7; Leshem in Josh. 19:47). They returned and reported to their brethren that this would be an easy town to conquer and in which to relocate. Six hundred fighting men then departed for the town, but on their way they persuaded a renegade Levite in Ephraim to join them, and he brought along a graven image from the house of Micah, his former employer. The small army then smote the town of Laish, which received no help from its ally, Sidon (Jud. 18:27–28). Having renamed the town Dan, they "set up the carved image; and Jonathan, the son of Gershom, the son of Manasseh, he and his sons were priests to the tribe of Dan until the day of the captivity of the land" (v. 30). This dismal spectacle of avarice combined with homemade idolatry indicates the inroads that the "serpent" had begun to make into this tribe. Dan became a cult center for idolatrous worship.

Two hundred years later, when Jeroboam rebelled against Rehoboam and split the kingdom into northern and southern divisions, he officially promoted idolatry as a means of preventing pilgrimages south to Jerusalem. "Whereupon the king took counsel, and made two calves of gold, and said unto them, It is too much for you to go up to Jerusalem; behold thy gods, O Israel, which brought thee up out of the land of Egypt. And he set the one in Bethel, and the other put he in Dan. And this thing became a sin; for the people went to worship before the one, even unto Dan" (1 Ki. 12:28–30). Another 200 years later, following an outward reformation under Jehu, idolatry still reigned in Dan. "Howbeit, from the sins of Jeroboam, the son of Nebat, who made Israel to sin, Jehu departed not from after them, to wit, the golden calves that were in Bethel, and that were in Dan" (2 Ki. 10:29).

The Lord's estimation of Dan and his idolatry can be seen in the decreasing role of the tribe in scriptural history. In the 20 different listings of the tribes, Dan is generally far down and often is the last in the list. Consider, for example, the order of march in the wilderness: "And the standard of the camp of the children of Dan set forward, which was the rear guard of all the camps throughout their hosts; and over its host was Ahiezer, the son of Ammishaddai" (Num. 10:25). Dan was the last tribe to receive its inheritance in the Promised Land (Josh. 19:47–49). Most striking is the total omission of Dan from the extensive tribal genealogies of 1 Chronicles 2—10! These scriptural facts should be remembered when facing the often-asked question of why Dan is omitted in the 144,000 Jews sealed in the Tribulation period (Rev. 7:4–8). Evidently this is due to the problem of idolatry which plagued this tribe throughout its history.

Two more facts also should be considered. First, the idea that the Antichrist will arise from this tribe is without clear scriptural basis. Since the Antichrist will originate from the 10-nation confederacy of Gentile nations (Dan. 2; 7; Rev. 13; 17), he most likely will be a Gentile rather than a Jew (he will be an anti-Messiah and not a false Messiah). Second, Dan does receive a tribal inheritance in the Millennial Kingdom (Ezek. 48:1–2). A more detailed consideration of these passages will be given in a later chapter.

A FERVENT PRAYER

Jacob closed his prophecy by turning his attention from Dan to the Lord himself: "I have waited for thy salvation, O LORD" (Gen. 49:18). Although this fervent prayer at first seems to be unrelated to the context, a closer examination reveals how appropriate it is. After pondering the varied fortunes of Dan with the tribe's propensity toward idolatry, Jacob expressed his longing for God's ultimate act of deliverance from all spiritual ills—salvation. Perhaps his reference to the "serpent" and the "heel" reminded him of the original promise of a deliverer given in Genesis 3:15: "And I will put enmity between thee and the woman, and between thy seed and her seed; he shall bruise thy head, and thou shalt bruise his heel."

Genesis 49:18 is the first of 78 occurrences of the word *salvation* in the Hebrew Scriptures. This word always refers to God's deliverance or salvation of His people through supernatural means. The Hebrew word for salvation is *yeshua*. The word is especially prominent in the Psalms and Isaiah. Consider Isaiah 12:2–3: "Behold, God is my salvation [Yeshua]; I will trust, and not be afraid; for the LORD, even the LORD, is my strength and my song; he also is become my salvation. Therefore, with joy shall ye draw water out of the wells of salvation [Yeshua]." Sometimes the Lord becomes so identified with the salvation He provides that the word becomes synonymous with His Messiah, the One who is salvation personified. "And he said, It is a light thing that thou shouldest be my servant to raise up the tribes of Jacob, and to restore the preserved of Israel; I will also give thee for a light to the nations, that thou mayest be my salvation [Yeshua] unto the end of the earth" (49:6). This is particularly clear in Isaiah 62:11: "Behold, the LORD hath proclaimed unto the end of the earth: Say ye to the daughter of Zion,

Behold, thy salvation [Yeshua] cometh; behold, his reward is with him, and his work before him."

Thus, Jacob was praying for more than just an impersonal deliverance; he was expressing his longing for a personal deliverer—Him whose name is Yeshua! This is in accord with Jewish tradition, as evidenced in the Jerusalem Targum, an ancient Aramaic translation of the Bible, and its paraphrased rendering of this verse: "My soul waiteth not for the deliverance of Gideon, for it was only temporal; nor for that deliverance of Samson, for it was transient; but for the redemption by the Messiah, Son of David, which in thy word thou has promised to send to thy people, Israel; for this, Thy Salvation [Yeshua], my soul waiteth."

Jacob's prayer of longing was finally answered, as clearly shown in the angel's message to Joseph recorded in Matthew 1:21: "And she shall bring forth a son, and thou shalt call his name JESUS [Yeshua in Hebrew]; for he shall save his people from their sins." That other Jews recognized in this child the fulfillment of Israel's longing for salvation is evident from the prayer of the aged Simeon when he held the young child, "Lord, now lettest thou thy servant depart in peace, according to thy word; for mine eyes have seen thy salvation [Yeshua in Hebrew], which thou has prepared before the face of all people; a light to lighten the Gentiles, and the glory of thy people, Israel" (Lk. 2:29–32).

It was no accident that the child born in fulfillment of many Hebrew prophecies was given the name Yeshua. He provided salvation, deliverance from the greatest captivity, that of sin's bondage. To all who place their faith in His person and work, real and lasting *yeshua*, or salvation, is given.

CHAPTER SEVEN

Gad, Asher, and Naphtali

Warrior, Provider, and Communicator

The aged Jacob followed the prophecy on his son Dan (Gen. 49:16–18) with three brief but significant words about the other three sons of the handmaids, Bilhah and Zilpah: Gad (v. 19), Asher (v. 20), and Naphtali (v. 21).

> *Gad, a troop shall overcome him; but he shall overcome at the last* (v. 19).

The English versions of the Scriptures cannot adequately catch the word play in this statement. Four of the six Hebrew words in this verse are some form of the word *Gad*. The following rendering most closely catches the meaning: "Gad, a troop shall troop upon him, but he shall troop on their heels."

This passage succinctly prophesies that the tribe of Gad will be harassed by bands of hostile enemies but will eventually repel their advances. A map of Israel in biblical times vividly displays the precarious position of Gad in relation to some of Israel's ancient enemies. Gad, along with Reuben and half of Manasseh, was allotted a portion of the land on the east side of the Jordan River (Josh. 13:24–28). Hostile bands of Ammonites and Moabites bordered his territory. The geographical name for this area was Gilead—a name in the Old Testament that often stood for the tribe of Gad (Jud. 5:17). The book of Judges portrays their perilous existence: "And that year they [the Philistines] vexed and oppressed the children of Israel—eighteen years, all the children of Israel who were on the other side of the Jordan in the land of the Amorites, which is in Gilead [i.e., Gad]" (Jud. 10:8; see also Jer. 49:1).

This constant exposure to hostile enemies resulted in Gad's developing a reputation as fierce warriors, constantly ready to defend their land. In David's days as a fugitive from Saul, the Gadite warriors who joined him at Ziklag were described in the following way: "And of the Gadites there separated themselves unto David into the stronghold in the wilderness, men of might, and men of war fit for the battle, that could handle shield and buckler, whose faces were like the faces of lions, and who were as swift as the roes upon the mountains" (1 Chr. 12:8; see also 1 Chr. 5:18–20). Moses' blessing on Gad also describes his ferocity: "And of Gad he said, Blessed be he who enlargeth Gad; he dwelleth like a lion, and teareth the arm with the crown of the head" (Dt. 33:20).

Scripture mentions nothing about any prominent individuals in this small but strategically located tribe. The most famous Gadite mentioned in the Old Testament was Jair who "judged Israel twenty and two years" (Jud. 10:3–5). Some have considered Jephthah, the "mighty man of valor," to be of this tribe since he is called a "Gileadite" in Judges 11:1. Certainly his military ability was characteristic of the tribe of Gad. In Jewish tradition, Elijah the prophet also was from this tribe.

Though little is mentioned of the tribe of Gad in the Bible, the lessons to be learned from them are many. Gad graduated from the proverbial school of hard knocks. His difficult experiences produced a toughness that only hard times can bring. The spiritual lesson gleaned from Gad is that in the furnace of affliction we are prepared to come forth as gold. Some of the most profitable lessons about suffering and adversity are learned, not in the classroom, but by undergoing the experience of suffering itself. The psalmist testifies, "It is good for me that I have been afflicted, that I might learn thy statutes" (Ps. 119:71).

Furthermore, Gad's constant readiness teaches us of the spiritual preparedness necessary to face the spiritual foe. Gad, much like his modern Israeli descendants, was constantly ready to face hostile neighbors. Peter reminds us of a similar danger that continually lurks around us: "Be sober, be vigilant, because your adversary, the devil, like a roaring lion walketh about, seeking whom he may devour" (1 Pet. 5:8). Believers never can afford to be without the armor God has provided lest we be caught off guard by one of Satan's fiery darts (cf. Eph. 6:10–17).

Finally, the promise to Gad is that "he shall overcome at the last" (Gen. 49:19). The seven churches of The Revelation each received a promise to the overcomer (Rev. 2:7, 11, 17, 26; 3:5, 12, 21). The overcomer is defined by John as follows: "For whatever is born of God overcometh the world; and this is the victory that overcometh the world, even our faith. Who is he that overcometh the world, but he that believeth that Jesus is the Son of God?" (1 Jn. 5:4–5). Whatever trials are faced by believers, we can rest assured that "in all these things we are more than conquerors through him that loved us" (Rom. 8:37).

Out of Asher his bread shall be fat and he shall yield royal dainties (Gen. 49:20).

Asher was the eighth of Jacob's sons, the second born to Zilpah, and the full brother of Gad (35:26). At his birth Leah exclaimed, "Happy am I, for the daughters will call me blessed: and she called his name Asher [i.e., happy]" (30:13). This foreshadowing of good fortune for Asher is repeated in Jacob's blessing. Asher will enjoy the rich products of a fertile land, teeming with those things which contribute to the sustenance of life, and also will, from his ample produce, supply those tasty morsels which grace the tables of kings. During Solomon's time, each of the 12 tribes in turn provided the royal provisions for one month each year (1 Ki. 4:7). The kings must have looked forward with great anticipation to Asher's assigned month, since he was known for his excellent gourmet delights.

Evidently, Asher sacrificed any military capability for his agricultural fame. According to Judges 1:31–32, the tribe never dislodged the Canaanite/Phoenician inhabitants of the northwestern coast of Israel. No judge, leader or military hero sprang from Asher. The most famous Asherite in the Bible was Anna, the prophetess who greeted the infant Jesus in the Temple (Lk. 2:36–38). This brief reference is evidence, however, that Jews of our Lord's time still maintained their tribal identity. Anna also provides evidence that representatives of the 10 northern tribes still existed over 700 years after the Assyrian captivity. In other words, the 10 tribes were not really lost as they are often described.

The word translated "fat" in Genesis 49:20 is the feminine form of the word for oil (*shemen*). This promise regarding oil was elaborated on by Moses in his later remark about Asher: "and let him dip his foot in oil [i.e., shemen]" (Dt. 33:24).

Some recent popularly written publications have sought to prove from these statements that Jacob and Moses were referring to petroleum oil. On the basis of these texts, an American Christian has actually been drilling for oil on Mount Carmel for a few years but, as of this writing, has come up dry.

While the discovery of oil in Israel would help substantially in easing the financial situation of that country, certain factors should cause us to be hesitant about making such claims based on these biblical texts. The oil mentioned in Genesis 49:20 and Deuteronomy 33:24 is not petroleum oil but olive oil. The word *shemen* appears 190 times in the Hebrew Scriptures, and all authoritative Hebrew lexicons define it as "olive oil." *The Theological Wordbook of the Old Testament* states, "shemen is the general word for olive oil in its various uses." This olive oil had an abundance of uses in biblical times (i.e., cooking [1 Ki. 17:16], lighting [Ex. 25:6], medicine [Ezek. 16:9], and religious anointing [Ex. 25:6]).

Furthermore, there is serious doubt that Mount Carmel was part of the ancient tribal territory of Asher. The most authoritative atlas of Bible lands available today locates the southern boundary of Asher at the foot of Mount Carmel (*Macmillan Bible Atlas*, map #72).

That Genesis 49:20 and Deuteronomy 33:24 refer to olive oil is confirmed by their fulfillment in history. The territory of Asher has always been known for its vast olive groves. Even today, most of the olive oil produced in Israel comes from Asher's territory. One of the fertile valleys in Asher's territory is actually called "The Valley of the Olive."

The lesson of Asher's prophecy is not that God will take care of Israel by a latter-day discovery of petroleum on Mount Carmel. God will take care of Israel in His own way. Investments of our money to drill oil wells based on questionable biblical interpretations are not wise methods through which to show our support for Israel.

The lesson of this prophecy is that Asher will be blessed with an abundance which he will share with others. The apostle Paul expressed it this way: "Let him that stole steal no more but, rather, let him labor, working with his hands the thing which is good, that he may have to give to him that needeth" (Eph. 4:28). We are to share with others that with which God has blessed us, not hoard it for ourselves (Lk. 16:9–12; 1 Tim. 6:16–18). Furthermore, the fruitfulness of Asher is associated with oil, which is often a scriptural symbol of the Holy Spirit. In a similar way, believers today are to bear fruit—the fruit of the Holy Spirit (Gal. 5:22–23).

Naphtali is a hind let loose; he giveth beautiful words (Gen. 49:21).

One again, an animal is mentioned in Jacob's blessings. *Hind* is the word used in the King James Version for a female deer, or doe, just as *hart* is used for the male deer, or buck (see Ps. 42:1; Isa. 35:6).

The fleetness and surety of foot seen in the hind is mentioned often in Scripture. Consider, for example, David's acknowledgment of God's help during his flight from Saul: "He maketh my feet like hinds' feet, and setteth me upon my high places" (Ps. 18:33). No doubt David had observed the hind as she fled from hunters in the desolate and savage wilderness where David also was fleeing from his hunter, Saul.

Jacob's prophecy is that Naphtali will be characterized by the speed and agility of a doe. In Jewish tradition, the son Naphtali was a very swift runner. He supposedly ran all the way from Egypt to Israel carrying the news to the aged Jacob that Joseph was still alive. The prophecy, however, refers primarily to the swiftness characteristic of the tribe of Naphtali. Since the latter part of the verse speaks of the "beautiful words" to be spoken by Naphtali, many interpreters see its fulfillment in the beautiful "Song of Deborah and Barak" recorded in Judges 5:1–31. There some of the tribes were distinguished for their heroic deeds during the battle with Jabin's Canaanite forces. It is interesting to note that Barak was from the tribe of Naphtali (Jud. 4:6), and the tribe is singled out in the song because of its special bravery. "Zebulun and Naphtali were a people who jeoparded their lives unto the death in the high places of the field" (5:18). The great battle between the Israelite and Canaanite forces described in Judges 4 prompted the tribes to send volunteers. While such tribes as Reuben, Dan, and Asher refused to send their contingents, tribes such as Naphtali were swift to rush their troops to battle. Where are we in the great spiritual battle being waged for the souls of men? Are we sitting in the grandstand or are we on the battlefield laying down our lives, if need be, as the swift warriors of

Naphtali were willing to do?

There is another possible application of this interesting prophecy. When Jesus began His ministry in Galilee, Matthew 4:13–15 states that He called His disciples in the very region of the tribe of Naphtali; hence, most of His disciples were from the area allotted to this ancient tribe. Is it possible that these early disciples carried the "beautiful words" of the gospel swiftly as hinds that were "let loose"?

The feet of the hind are swift. The book of Romans speaks about two different types of feet. Romans 3:15 condemns the feet that "are swift to shed blood"; while, on the other hand, Romans 10:15 commends those who preach the gospel with these words: "How beautiful are the feet of them that preach the gospel of peace, and bring glad tidings of good things!" What a contrast, and what a lesson to those of us who are followers of Jesus. Are our feet as swift to tell someone about the gospel as they are to share some damaging gossip?

These three short prophecies tell us much about Gad, Asher, and Naphtali and say much which is profitable to us today. The lesson from Gad: Be ready. The lesson from Asher: Be fruitful. The lesson from Naphtali: Be swift.

CHAPTER EIGHT

Joseph

Faithful and Fruitful

Joseph is a fruitful bough, even a fruitful bough by a well, whose branches run over the wall. The archers have harassed him, and shot at him, and hated him; but his bow abode in strength, and the arms of his hands were made strong by the hands of the mighty God of Jacob (from there is the shepherd, the stone of Israel), even by the God of thy father, who shall help thee; and by the Almighty, who shall bless thee with blessings of heaven above, blessings of the deep that lieth under, blessings of the breasts, and of the womb. The blessings of thy father have prevailed above the blessings of my progenitors unto the utmost bound of the everlasting hills: they shall be on the head of Joseph, and on the crown of the head of him that was separate from his brethren (Gen. 49:22–26).

A s the aged, bedridden Jacob pronounced prophetic blessings on his sons by Leah, Bilhah, and Zilpah, he must have looked forward with great anticipation to what God had in store for his two youngest sons—Joseph and Benjamin. These were the sons of his first love, the wife for whom he had worked so long, his beloved Rachel.

Rachel had been barren for many years while her sisterly rival, Leah, had given Jacob six sons! Although her hand maid Bilhah (according to the custom of those days) had provided Jacob with two sons, Rachel still longed for children of her own flesh and blood. In desperation, she cried out to Jacob, "Give me children, or else I die" (Gen. 30:1). In tender mercy, God responded to her cries of longing. "And God remembered Rachel, and God hearkened to her, and opened her womb. And she conceived, and bore a son; and said, God hath taken away my reproach: And she called his name Joseph; and said, The LORD shall add to me another son" (vv. 22–24). The Hebrew meaning of the name *Joseph* is "may He add." In other words, while Rachel certainly was thankful for this son, she desired at least one more! God also granted that request when she gave birth to Benjamin shortly before her death (cf. Gen. 35:16–18).

A LOOK BACK

Jacob's initial words to Joseph strike the keynote of this entire oracle, which is the longest in this marvelous series of prophecies. "Joseph is a fruitful bough, even a fruitful bough by a well, whose branches run over the wall" (49:22). Fruitfulness marked Joseph's life (vv. 22–24), and it would also characterize his descendants (vv. 25–26).

The reference to Joseph as a "fruitful bough" (efforts of some modern translations to make him a "wild colt" have a poor linguistic and contextual basis) recalls Joseph's own remark recorded in Genesis 41:52, "And the name of the second son called he Ephraim: For God hath caused me to be fruitful in the land of my affliction." In spite of the numerous obstacles placed in his path, Joseph was faithful and fruitful in overcoming each one.

Many writers have noted some interesting parallels between Joseph's experiences and events in the life of the Lord Jesus. Consider the following that have been mentioned in many sermons and devotional studies. (1) Joseph was the delight of his father (Gen. 37:3); Jesus was the "beloved Son" of His Father (Mt. 3:17). (2) Joseph was rejected by his brothers (Gen. 37:4, e.g,); Jesus' "own" did not receive Him (Jn. 1:11; 7:5). (3) Joseph was sold into Egypt (Gen. 37:28); Jesus fled there with His parents under duress (Mt. 2:14–15). (4) Joseph withstood temptation to sin (Gen. 39:7–12); Jesus withstood Satan's temptations (Mt. 4:1–11). (5) Joseph was raised from the death of prison and exalted to the side of Pharaoh (Gen. 41:14–43); Jesus was raised from the dead and exalted to His Father's right hand (Acts 2:32–33). (6) Joseph mercifully forgave his brothers for causing him to suffer (Gen. 50:15–21); Jesus prayed that the Father would forgive those responsible for His suffering (Lk. 23:34). (7) Joseph took a Gentile bride (Gen. 41:45); Jesus is calling out Gentiles to be part of His bride (Col. 1:24–27).

Although these parallels appear striking, they should not be over-emphasized. It is significant that the New Testament never mentions Joseph as a type of Christ. This is not final proof that Joseph is not a type of Christ, but it should prevent us from dogmatically stating that he is so. Furthermore, an emphasis on typology tends to obscure the real and vital lesson that Joseph has for all readers (i.e., he trusted God in the midst of his trials).

When Jacob looked back at his son's life, it is this important lesson which he mentions. "The archers have harassed him, and shot at him, and hated him; but his bow abode in strength, and the arms of his hands were made strong by the hands of the mighty God of Jacob (from there is the shepherd, the stone of Israel)" (Gen. 49:23-24). In spite of Joseph's suffering at the hands of his brothers, his trust in God was unswerving. The Genesis commentator, George Bush, aptly observes:

> *The prophecy here points to Joseph in person, from whose history its fulfillment appears evident. He was aimed and shot at, as it were, by the bitter and reviling words of his brethren, and still more deeply wounded by their cruel treatment. He was sold into Egypt through envy, and imprisoned by a lie. His virtue was violently assaulted by his mistress, his innocence wronged by his master, and his patience severely tried by the ingratitude of a fellow prisoner. Yet "his bow abode in strength." The divine favor forsook him not.*[1]

The source of Joseph's strength was his knowledge of the true God. Five different titles of the Lord are mentioned in this passage. Each illustrates some aspect of His character: "the mighty God of Jacob," "the shepherd," "the stone of Israel" (v. 24), the "God [El] of thy father," and "the Almighty" (v. 25). Although each of these titles bears out much precious truth, consider only the last one—"Almighty." The Hebrew word is *Shaddai*, which carries the idea of All-Sufficient One or Sustainer. It is formed from the Hebrew word for a mother's breast (*shad*), which nourishes and sustains the child. In the same way, God sustained Joseph in his weaknesses. It is also interesting to note that when Jacob described the abundant blessings on Joseph, he carefully mentioned "blessings of the breasts" (shad).

Because of his intimate knowledge of God, Joseph was able to discern His hand even in his personal setbacks. When he finally revealed his identity to his brothers, he told them,

> *Now therefore be not grieved, nor angry with yourselves, that ye sold me here; for God did send me before you to preserve life. And God sent me before you to preserve you a posterity in the earth, and to save your lives by a great deliverance. So now it was not you that sent me here, but God: and he hath made me a father to Pharaoh, and lord of all his house, and a ruler throughout all the land of Egypt* (45:5, 7–8).

It is striking to consider that almost every time Joseph speaks, he mentions God. Such a God-filled life will also lead us to discern God's hand even in our trials and troubles—to perceive His purpose and leading even in the difficult circumstances which we all encounter. This is the real lesson for us from the life of Joseph.

A LOOK AHEAD

The remainder of Jacob's prophecy looks forward to the blessings to be experienced by the tribe of Joseph. "The blessings of thy father have prevailed above the blessings of my progenitors unto the utmost bound of the everlasting hills: they shall be on the head of Joseph, and on the crown of the head of him that was separate from his brethren" (49:26). The words *bless* or *blessings* appear six times in verses 25 and 26. These blessings are placed squarely on Joseph's head, "the head of him that was separate from his brethren." The word *separate* is *nazir*, which is used later to describe one who took a Nazirite vow to be separated from the vine and from dead bodies as well as to refrain from cutting his hair (Num. 6:2–21). The use of the word here, however, recalls the long period of time during which God set Joseph apart from his brothers and advanced him to preeminence over them.

It is obvious that the patriarchal blessing, normally reserved for the firstborn, instead was imparted to Joseph. Reuben, due to his incest with Bilhah, had forfeited both his leadership role to Judah and his father's double blessing to Joseph (Gen. 49:3–4), as is clearly stated in

1 Chronicles 5:1–2. Further more, according to Deuteronomy 21:17, the privilege of the firstborn was to receive a double portion of the inheritance, a portion twice as large as that of each of his brothers. Since Joseph received the blessing of the firstborn instead of Reuben, what effect did this have on his descendants?

When he became established in Egypt, Joseph and his wife Asenath had two sons, Manasseh and Ephraim (cf. Gen. 41:50–52). When Jacob had been in Egypt 17 years, Joseph and his two sons visited him as he lay on his sickbed. In the touching scene recorded in Genesis 48:1–22, Jacob actually adopted Ephraim and Manasseh as his own, elevating them to the position of his other sons. He told Joseph, "And now thy two sons, Ephraim and Manasseh, who were born unto thee in the land of Egypt before I came unto thee into Egypt, are mine; as Reuben and Simeon, they shall be mine" (48:5). Therefore, the double blessing on Joseph meant that instead of producing one tribe, he would produce two! From that time forward, the lists of the tribes normally mention the tribes of Ephraim and Manasseh, rather than the tribe of Joseph. To be exact, tribal lists appear 16 times in the Bible after Genesis, and Joseph is mentioned only three times, his place usually taken by Ephraim and Manasseh.

The great fruitfulness of these tribes is illustrated in the two census calculations taken at the beginning and end of the wilderness wandering. In Numbers 1, the total population of Ephraim and Manasseh (i.e., the tribe of Joseph) is 75,900, compared to the 74,600 of the next largest tribe, Judah. In Numbers 26, their total population was 85,200 while Judah's was 76,500. Jacob prophesied that the tribes of Ephraim and Manasseh would "grow into a multitude in the midst of the earth" (Gen. 48:16). He even wittingly switched his right hand to the head of the younger and prophesied that Ephraim would be greater than his older brother Manasseh, following a pattern practiced earlier in Genesis (vv. 17–19). Manasseh was great in that his descendants had the largest land allotment of any tribe, actually settling on both sides of the Jordan with an eastern and a western branch. Ephraim, however, produced greater individuals (i.e., Joshua, Moses' successor). The prominence of Ephraim is illustrated by the fact that the entire northern kingdom often was called by that name alone in many of the later prophets (consider Hos. 11:3; 12:1; Jer. 31:9, 20).

An effort has been made by some to identify England and America as the modern tribes of Manasseh and Ephraim and thus the recipients of these promises. This teaching of British-Israelism, which began in the 19th century, is now a doctrinal plank of many cults and white supremacist groups. Based on questionable exegesis of isolated texts and discredited by dubious historical identifications, this movement is but one of many seeking to answer the question of the whereabouts of the so-called 10 lost tribes. A later chapter will explore in detail this fascinating subject and offer some alternative suggestions. Suffice it now to say that we need look no further than the scriptural history of the tribes of Ephraim and Manasseh to find the fulfillments of these promises of blessing and fruitfulness.

After meditating on the faithful life and fruitfulness of Joseph, one final lesson emerges. Joseph is a convincing example of the truth stated in 1 Peter 5:6: "Humble yourselves, therefore, under the mighty hand of God, that he may exalt you in due time." Humanly speaking, it must have been extremely difficult to wait for God's timing after having been unjustly sold as a slave, unjustly imprisoned for remaining pure and unjustly forgotten by an acquaintance whom he had helped. Most of us would have cried out, Why me? Yet, Joseph waited on God during his trials without seeking either revenge or advancement. Finally, in His timing, God exalted His faithful servant and lifted him to a place of honor where he could be a blessing to others.

Our responsibility is not to be ambitious and self-seeking. It is to be faithful. His job is to hand out the promotions. Joseph faithfully waited in prison before he was lifted to the throne. Elijah faithfully waited at Cherith before he triumphed at Carmel. Moses faithfully labored in Midian before he challenged the power of Egypt. Jesus faithfully carried the cross before He wore the crown.

This is a principle of spiritual growth: "Thou hast been faithful over a few things, I will make thee ruler over many things" (Mt. 25:21, 23).

May this great lesson of Joseph's faithfulness in trial not be lost on our impatient and ambitious egos!

CHAPTER NINE

Benjamin

A Ravenous Wolf

Benjamin shall consume as a wolf; in the morning he shall devour the prey, and at night he shall divide the spoil (Gen. 49:27).

A wolf is the fifth animal used by Jacob to characterize the future activities of his sons' descendants. Jacob thus declared that Benjamin, his 12th and last son, would be characterized by a vicious and warlike attitude. It is a striking surprise to many that Jacob spoke in this manner about his youngest son of whom he was so fond. His words must have arisen from the Spirit of God rather than from the tender feelings which he undoubtedly had for young Benjamin. Matthew Henry eloquently declared, "It is plain that Jacob spoke by prophecy and not by natural affection, else he would have spoken with more tenderness of his beloved Benjamin."[1] Did Jacob's prophecy come true? Did Benjamin's descendants evidence a ravenous, wolf-like spirit? To answer these questions, we must examine the son Benjamin as well as the tribe Benjamin.

BENJAMIN THE SON

Benjamin was the 12th son of Jacob and the second son born to him by Rachel, his beloved and dearest wife. When Benjamin's older brother was born, he was named Joseph, which means "may He add"—a pious prayer that was granted when Joseph's younger brother was born. His birth, however, was an occasion of joy mingled with sorrow. Genesis 35:16–20 records the events:

> *And they journeyed from Bethel; and there was but a little way to come to Ephrath: and Rachel travailed, and she had hard labor. And it came to pass, when she was in hard labor, that the midwife said unto her, Fear not; thou shalt have this son also. And it came to pass, as her soul was in departing (for she died), that she called his name Benoni: but his father called him Benjamin. And Rachel died, and was buried in the way to Ephrath, which is Bethlehem. And Jacob set a pillar upon her grave: that is the pillar of Rachel's grave unto this day.*

As Rachel lay dying, her last act was to name her newborn son *Benoni*, meaning "son of my pain." Jacob, however, named the child *Benjamin*, meaning "right-hand son." This name proved to be prophetic as well, because Benjamin was later to replace the lost Joseph in Jacob's affection.

The events surrounding Joseph's being sold into Egypt and God's providence in his preservation and elevation were detailed in the previous chapter. When Jacob's favorite son was thus lost, he evidently bestowed all of his fatherly affection on Benjamin. For example, when the sons were sent down to Egypt during the famine to buy corn, Jacob kept Benjamin at home with him, "Lest perhaps mischief befall him" (42:4).

Later, when Joseph commanded that his brothers return home to bring the youngest, Jacob cried out, "Me have ye bereaved of my children; Joseph is not, and Simeon is not, and ye will take Benjamin away: all these things are against me" (v. 36). Still later, it was in Benjamin's sack that Joseph secretly had his cup placed as the brothers were leaving Egypt after having bought more grain (44:1–13). Although it may be overstating the case, one cannot help imagining young Benjamin as a pampered and protected Little Lord Fauntleroy type receiving all the doting affection of an aged father. Whether or not this characterization is accurate, the future history of Benjamin's descendants records nothing resembling perfumed sweetness.

BENJAMIN THE TRIBE

Jacob's prophecy that Benjamin would be "a wolf who tears in pieces" found graphic fulfillment throughout the history of that tribe. Before examples of Benjamin's ferocity are mentioned, however, the strategic location of the tribe should be noted. According to Joshua 18:11–28, Benjamin basically was allotted a buffer zone between the two dominant tribes of Judah and Ephraim. Its northern line was the same as Ephraim's southern border, and its southern line the same as Judah's northern boundary (see map). Benjamite territory included many cities important in biblical history (i.e., Jericho, Bethel, Gibeon, Ramah, and Mizpah). Most importantly, Jerusalem itself was in Benjamin, and not in Judah as is so often popularly conceived (Josh. 18:28). Many have seen a reference to Jerusalem in Moses' blessing on Benjamin, "And of Benjamin he said, The beloved of the LORD shall dwell in safety by him; and the LORD shall cover him all the day long, and he shall dwell between his shoulders" (Dt. 33:12). Thus, the Lord later located His sanctuary, the Temple, in Benjamite territory.

Jacob's prophecy stated that the "wolf" would devour his prey in the morning and divide its spoil in the evening (cf. Gen. 49:27). Compared to a wolf's predatory activity throughout the day, many ferocious Benjamites are recorded from the earliest to the latest periods of Israelite history.

The first evidence of this ferocity is seen in Ehud, the second judge of Israel (Jud. 3:12–30). This fearless warrior single-handedly assassinated Eglon, the king of the Moabites, who had been oppressing Israel for 18 years. Ehud's left-handedness, which was characteristic of Benjamites (Jud. 20:15–16), was a bit ironic since Benjamin means "right-hand son." Concealing his weapon under his garments on his right thigh (which is probably why it was undetected), Ehud gained entrance to Eglon's presence, ran the fat king through with his dagger, and escaped undetected. The resulting confusion led to a great Israelite victory over the Moabites and resulted in an 80-year period of peace.

The next evidence of Benjamin's ravenous character is one of the truly dark episodes in Israel's history. In the anarchic days when "every man did that which was right in his own eyes" (Jud. 17:6; 21:25), Benjamin was at the center of a devastating civil war among the tribes. Responding to the brutality of the Benjamite men of Gibeah (graphically described in Judges 19), the other tribes launched a disciplinary action against the entire tribe (chap. 20). When the tribal leaders refused to relinquish the guilty offenders, a major military confrontation resulted. Although greatly outnumbered, Benjamin, with their famous 700 left-handed stone slingers (20:16), inflicted 40,000 casualties on their brethren in the first two days of fighting. On the third day, however, the tide of battle turned and the forces of Benjamin were devastated nearly to the point of annihilation. Only 600 escaped, and these formed the nucleus of the continuing, although greatly weakened, tribe. The wolf had torn, but in the end it had been torn!

The next prominent member of the tribe of Benjamin, and probably its most famous representative, was Saul, son of Kish. The ferocity of his rule was evident to all, particularly his enemies. When the town of Jabesh-gilead was besieged by the Ammonites, Saul, probably due to family ties (cf. Jud. 21:12–14), dramatically mustered the armies of Israel and attacked the Ammonites by night "so that two of them were not left together" (1 Sam. 11:1–11). Saul's warlike rule was felt by many surrounding kingdoms, whom he not only defeated but also humiliated: "And wherever he turned himself, he defeated them" (14:47).

Saul's son Jonathan was also a great warrior, although his zeal was channeled for the Lord rather than his own glory, as was his father's. First Samuel 14 records the brilliant maneuver of Jonathan and his armor-bearer in climbing a sheer cliff and slaughtering a Philistine garrison of 20 soldiers. This bold deed led to complete confusion in the enemy camp and its eventual rout at the hands of the Israelite troops. Contrasted with his father's selfish zeal, Jonathan acted on faith in God's promise (14:6, 12). This godly "wolf" was doubtless one of those unnamed heroes of faith who, according to Hebrews 11:34, "became valiant in fight, and turned to flight the armies of the aliens."

Other ferocious Benjamites were: (1) Abner, Saul's cousin and commander of his army, who mercilessly killed Asahel and was himself murdered by Joab (2 Sam. 2:23; 3:30); (2) Shimei, who cursed David during his flight from Absalom and was himself killed by Solomon in return (16:5–13; 1 Ki. 2:44–46), and (3) Sheba, who led a rebellion against David and was himself beheaded by the citizens of Abel Beth-maacah (2 Sam. 20:1–22). These serve as examples of how selfish and misguided zeal receives its own punishment in the end.

In the evening of Israel's Old Testament history, however, there appeared two stellar examples of Benjamite zeal channeled for the glory of God. Esther and Mordecai, cousins in the Persian town of Shushan, were boldly instrumental in saving their own people and turning the tables on Haman and other Jew haters of that time (see Est. 7 and 9). The Jewish festival of Purim commemorates their brave zeal. In this unique way, Benjamin divided the spoil in fulfillment of Genesis 49:27.

Although this listing exhausts the major members of Benjamin cited in the Old Testament Scriptures, there remains one other member of this tribe who graphically portrayed the wolf-like viciousness of his ancestors. In one of his letters he wrote "I say, then, Hath God cast away his people? God forbid. For I also am an Israelite, of the seed of Abraham, of the tribe of Benjamin" (Rom. 11:1). In another letter, while summarizing his ancestry, he states that he was "Circumcised the eighth day, of the stock of Israel, of the tribe of Benjamin, an Hebrew of the Hebrews; as touching the law, a Pharisee" (Phil. 3:5). His parents called him Saul, after an ancient namesake, although we know him better by his Roman name, Paul. If ever there appeared on the pages of the Bible a prime example of a ferocious Benjamite wolf, it was this citizen of Tarsus who had boasted so proudly of his Pharisaic fervor and devotion to the traditions of his forefathers. His blind zeal was such that he attacked his own brethren who were following the Nazarene Messiah.

Consider the following quotations from his own hand: "For ye have heard of my manner of life in time past in the Jews' religion, how that beyond measure I persecuted the church of God, and wasted it" (Gal. 1:13); "And I persecuted this way unto the death; binding and delivering into prisons both men and women" (Acts 22:4); "I verily thought within myself, that I ought to do many things contrary to the name of Jesus of Nazareth, which thing I also did in Jerusalem; and many of the saints did I shut up in prison, having received authority from the chief priests. And when they were put to death, I gave my voice against them" (26:9–10).

Luke, the early church historian, described this son of Benjamin thus: "As for Saul, he made havoc of the church, entering into every house and, haling men and women, committed them to prison" (8:3); "And Saul, yet breathing out threatenings and slaughter against the disciples of the Lord, went unto the high priest, and desired of him letters to Damascus to the synagogues, that if he found any of this way, whether they were men or women, he might bring them bound unto Jerusalem" (9:1–2). This "wolf" tore in pieces the followers of Jesus until his activities were brought to a halt by the very One he was persecuting (9:4). From that day on, Saul was radically different. His zeal, however, did not abate—rather, it was channeled in a positive, God-honoring direction. Instead of attacking the followers of the Lord, he spent the rest of his earthly life assaulting the citadels of Satan! Matthew Henry has written graphically, "Blessed Paul was of this tribe and he did, in the morning of his day, devour the prey as a persecutor, but in the evening he divided the spoil as a preacher."

God can mold and utilize any temperament—whether it be phlegmatic, choleric, sanguine, or melancholy—when that person has surrendered completely to the Lord. God transformed the Benjamite Paul, not by drastically altering his temperament, but by refining and rechanneling his misguided zeal into a God-honoring direction.

Let us determine in our hearts to be clay in the Potter's hand, willing to be molded for His purposes. May God grant us a host of Benjamins who will tear in pieces the armies of darkness!

These Are the 12 Tribes of Israel

All these are the twelve tribes of Israel: and this is that which their father spoke unto them, and blessed them; every one, according to his blessing, he blessed them (Gen. 49:28).

In the foregoing chapters, we have studied the historical development of each tribe of Israel, utilizing the series of prophecies pronounced by Jacob upon his sons recorded in Genesis 49. The amazing agreement between the prophecies and their fulfillments indicates that the divine mind was behind the words uttered by the dying patriarch in the presence of his 12 sons. There are a few biblical passages, however, in which the tribes are viewed as an entire unit rather than as individual groups. These Scriptures merit some comment. Furthermore, a brief examination of the many Jewish legends attached to the tribes should provide some interesting insights in our consideration of these 12 sons and their descendants.

THE EPHOD AND THE BREASTPLATE

The garments of the Israelite high priest are described in detail in Exodus 28. Among those garments were an ephod and a breastplate. The 12 tribes of Israel were uniquely associated with both of these items.

The ephod was a cloth garment that hung over the shoulders and covered the front and back. Fastened to the shoulder pieces of the ephod and placed in gold settings were two onyx stones. On each of the stones were engraved "the names of the children of Israel: Six of their names on one stone, and the other six names of the rest on the other stone, according to their birth" (vv. 9–10). Thus, on one onyx stone were engraved the names of Reuben, Simeon, Levi, Judah, Dan, and Naphtali, while on the other stone were inscribed the names of Gad, Asher, Issachar, Zebulun, Joseph, and Benjamin. The inscription of their names on the stones coordinates with the order of their births; whereas in Genesis 49, the sequence in which the prophecies were given was determined by their respective mothers.

It is stated clearly that the purpose of the location of the onyx stones was so that "Aaron shall bear their names before the LORD upon his two shoulders for a memorial" (Ex. 28:12). Thus, the high priest represented all Israel when he ministered in the Tabernacle, particularly upon entering the Holy of Holies on Yom Kippur, the Day of Atonement (see Lev. 16).

A more detailed role for the tribal names is outlined with the description of the "breastplate of judgment" (Ex. 28:15–29). This seven-inch-square pouch, made of the same materials as the ephod, was attached to it by four gold rings. Inside the pouch were placed two precious stones called "Urim" and "Thummin" which were used in seeking God's will for decisions (see Lev. 8:8; Num. 27:31; Dt. 33:8; 1 Sam. 28:6). The Scriptures do not indicate how the stones accomplished this, but it is probable that one stone indicated a yes answer and the other no when pulled from the pouch at random by the high priest. Dogmatism on this point, however, should be avoided.

On the outside of the breastplate and placed in gold settings were 12 precious stones in four rows of three stones each. On each of the stones was inscribed the name of one of the tribes of Israel, presumably in the order of their births, as was the case with the onyx stones on the shoulders (Ex. 28:10). The order and names of the stones are listed in Exodus 28:17-20. The layout would appear as follows:

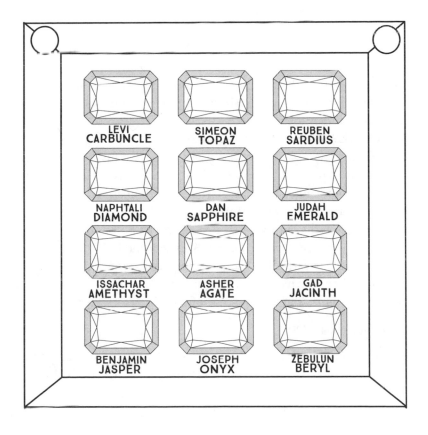

The reasoning behind this order is that Hebrew is written from right to left, making it logical that the sardius inscribed with the name of Reuben, the first son, would be in the upper right-hand corner. Furthermore, some of the names of the stones found in the Authorized Version may be more accurately identified today than in the early 17th century, when that excellent translation was made. For example, Hebrew scholars suggest that the word rendered sardius was a ruby, the carbuncle was a beryl, the emerald was a turquoise, the diamond an emerald and the beryl a chrysolite. The comment of George Bush, however, on the identity of the stones is most appropriate: "We are constrained to remark that after the research expended by antiquarians upon the subject much uncertainty still rests upon it. They cannot be dogmatically identified."[1]

We can, however, confidently affirm the reason these stones, engraved with the tribal names, were on the breast plate. Exodus 28:29 declares, "And Aaron shall bear the names of the children of Israel in the breastplate of judgment upon his heart, when he goeth in unto the holy place, for a memorial before the LORD continually." Thus, the nation as a whole rested on the high-priestly person and work (on his shoulders); on the other hand, he carried them individually and lovingly into God's presence (on his heart). "For Christ is not entered into the holy places made with hands, which are the figures of the true, but into heaven itself, now to appear in the presence of God for us" (Heb. 9:24).

THE TRIBAL ENCAMPMENT

As the tribes of Israel departed from Mount Sinai, they proceeded in a definite marching order with Judah as the vanguard (Num. 10:11–36). When the tribes stopped and set up camp around the Tabernacle, they again arranged themselves in a definite order.

In the middle of the camp stood the Tabernacle with the priests and Levites immediately around it. On the east side of the Tabernacle were the tribes of Judah, Issachar, and Zebulun; on the south side were Reuben, Simeon, and Gad; on the west side were Ephraim, Manasseh, and Benjamin; and on the north side were Dan, Asher, and Naphtali.

The encampment of the tribes of Israel, as described in Numbers 2:1–31 and 10:11–33 would appear as follows:

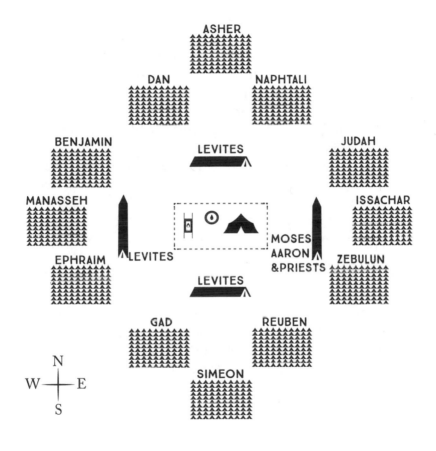

This arrangement of Jacob's descendants may appear, at first glance, to be without any purpose. Upon closer examination, however, it can be observed that the three tribes in each set of three were the nearest related by blood to each other. Since Levi was not included in the four sets, Gad, who was born through the maid of Levi's mother, took his place alongside Levi's closest brothers, Simeon and Reuben.

Each set of three, furthermore, was led by the most prominent tribe of that group—Judah, Reuben, Ephraim, and Dan. In three of the cases, this was because the tribal founder was the oldest of the three brothers. Ephraim, however, was placed ahead of his older brother, Manasseh. Thus, Jacob's prophecy about Ephraim being greater than Manasseh was already finding its fulfillment (Gen. 48:19–20).

An interesting feature of this camp was that a standard or banner was placed on the four sides beside the prominent tribe of each triad. No further information is provided about the size, color, or representation on these standards. Jewish tradition, however, does provide a clue to the way in which later generations of Jews viewed the standards. The Aramaic paraphrase of the Torah, called *Targum Jonathan*, and the ancient commentary on Numbers, called *Bemidbar Rabbah*, suggest that each tribe assigned a color corresponding to the color of its respective stone in the high priest's breastplate. Thus, the color of Dan would be blue because a sapphire is blue. The four standards, therefore, were composed of the colors of the three tribes of each triad. The tradition continues that each of the four standards depicted a living being. Judah's animal was a lion, Reuben's a man, Ephraim's an ox, and Dan's an eagle. This tradition may have been influenced by the cherubim in Ezekiel's vision who also had four faces (Ezek. 1:10; see also Rev. 4:7). It should be emphasized that there is no solid biblical or historical basis for these descriptions of the standards. The Jewish tradition, however, does provide the most logical suggestion for their descriptions, particularly in the case of Judah and Ephraim (see Gen. 49:9 and Dt. 33:17).

Jewish tradition can be helpful in reflecting on a biblical passage, but at times it can be misleading. In the previously mentioned *Targum Jonathan*, it is suggested that the 12 signs of the zodiac correspond to the standards of the 12 tribes! Judah the lion, therefore, corresponds to Leo, while Ephraim and Manasseh are Taurus the bull! It is astounding that pagan Babylonian astrology could have penetrated in such a way into some of the ancient holy books of the Jews. The visitor to Israel, for example, is perplexed when he views the uncovered remains of some ancient synagogues revealing large mosaic floors emblazoned with zodiacal signs alongside each tribal name! This is further evidence that the worldly influence of Hellenism had penetrated deeply into some strata of Judaism despite the clear warnings against astrology in the Hebrew Scriptures (e.g., Isa. 47:12–14).

The orderly arrangements of the stones on the high priest's breastplate and Israel's wilderness encampment do not teach extreme and sensational lessons. Exodus 28 and Numbers 2, however, remind us that the ordered plan of God for His people was conceived and executed by the One whose wisdom is far above the heavens. The breastplate was worn by the representative of the people—the high priest. Just as Aaron entered into the inner sanctuary with the tribal names on his breast and shoulders, so the Messiah entered once into the Holy Place with His own blood which He shed for all those who trust Him and are part of His eternal purpose (Heb. 9:11–12). Just as the sanctuary, God's dwelling place, was in the center of the Israelite camp, so today the Lord dwells spiritually in the midst of His people—all of whom, individually, are joined together, collectively, as part of His eternal and spiritual temple.

"Oh, the depth of the riches both of the wisdom and knowledge of God! How unsearchable are his judgments, and his ways past finding out!" (Rom. 11:33).

CHAPTER ELEVEN

Will the 10 Lost Tribes Ever Be Found?

In December, 1984, astounding news leaked to the world press. For over a year, the Israeli government had been secretly flying more than 10,000 Ethiopian Jews out of their refugee camps in the Sudan to their new homes in the modern State of Israel. The Beta Israel, as they call themselves (*Falashas* in the Ethiopian language), claim that their Judaic faith originated after the Queen of Sheba returned from her famous visit to King Solomon, bringing with her the knowledge of the one true God. Rabbis in Israel, however, had another explanation—these Ethiopian Jews were descendants of the tribe of Dan, one of the mysterious lost tribes of Israel.

In a recent edition of a Jewish newspaper, an article appeared describing the Jewish customs of the Pashtu—an Islamic tribe in Afghanistan. They circumcise their sons on the eighth day, wear four-cornered garments, perform levirate marriages, and don traditional sidelocks and beards. These customs have convinced some researchers that the Pashta tribe is a remnant of the 10 lost tribes of Israel.

In a far different vein, a prominent American radio and TV "evangelist" proclaimed for years that the 10 lost tribes were not lost but had reappeared as the British and American peoples, whom, he claimed, were the inheritors of the promises to ancient Israel!

These various ideas appearing in the 20th century have again raised some important questions in the minds of many: What did happen to the 10 tribes? Have some of them survived until today? Can we identify these tribes with any of the many ethnic groups living on planet Earth today? This chapter will attempt to answer these and other questions about the lost tribes by sifting through the myths and ideas of men to ascertain the scriptural and historical truth about the so-called lost tribes.

THE MEANING OF THE PHRASE "10 LOST TRIBES"

In 930 BC, soon after the death of Solomon, the united kingdom of Israel was ruptured into two separate kingdoms, generally referred to in Scripture as the northern kingdom of Israel and the southern kingdom of Judah. Both of these kingdoms failed in their stand against idolatry, were eventually conquered by foreign powers and ceased to be independent kingdoms. The northern kingdom, consisting of 10 tribal allotments, succumbed to the Assyrians around 721 BC, "For the children of Israel walked in all the sins of Jeroboam which he did; they departed not from them, until the LORD removed Israel out of his sight, as he had said by all his servants, the prophets. So was Israel carried away out of their own land to Assyria unto this day" (2 Ki. 17:22–23).

Their southern brethren, the kingdom of Judah, consisting primarily of the tribal allotments of Judah and Benjamin, were conquered by the Babylonians in 586 BC. Some of these exiles returned under Zerubbabel and reestablished their existence in 536 BC.

Since, however, there never was a formal return of the northern tribes to reestablish their kingdom, they have been popularly referred to as the 10 lost tribes.

IDEAS ABOUT THE IDENTITY OF THE 10 LOST TRIBES

The television series "In Search of . . ." is an indication of how fascinated people are about the unanswered questions surrounding the mysterious, the unknown, and the unexplained. The subsequent history of the remnants of the northern kingdom has fueled the imagination of many travelers, writers, romanticists, and cultists. There are three basic ideas that have emerged about their identity.

First, one traditional Jewish explanation is that the 10 tribes are forever lost, assimilated among their Assyrian captors, and never again will be found. The great second-century rabbi Akiba expressed this opinion strongly: "The ten tribes shall not return again—they have completely disappeared" (Mishna Sanhedrin 10:3). This, however, seems to be a minority opinion among the rabbis in the Talmud.

Second, another Jewish tradition is that the tribes continued to exist beyond the mysterious river Sambatyon whose rapidly flowing waters prevented their crossing it. The Jewish historian Josephus stated at the end of the first century, "The ten tribes are beyond the Euphrates till now, and are an immense multitude and not to be estimated in numbers" (Antiquities 11:133). Throughout the Middle Ages, various pseudo-messiahs, such as David Reubeni, appeared in Europe and claimed to be from a Jewish kingdom composed of the 10 lost tribes. Legends circulated that fired the hope of their soon discovery, but no tangible evidence of their existence was ever produced. It was this tradition that motivated Israel's rabbis to declare that the Jews of Ethiopia belong to the lost tribe of Dan.

Third, theories abound which identify various ethnic groups today as being the descendants of the 10 lost tribes. *The Encyclopedia Judaica* states, "There is hardly a people, from the Japanese to the British, and from the Red Indians to the Afghans, who have not been suggested, and hardly a place, among them Africa, India, China, Persia, Kurdistan, Caucasia, the United States, and Great Britain" (Vol. 15, p. 1006).

The theory attempting to explain the subsequent history of the 10 lost tribes that has gained the greatest following is the view known as British-Israelism. First propounded in 19th-century England, the basic premise of British-Israelism is that the 10 tribes captured by the Assyrians are, in reality, the Saxae, or Scythians, who surged westward through Northern Europe and eventually became the ancestors of the Saxons who invaded England. The theory maintains that the Anglo-Saxons are thus the Israel of the Bible.

Therefore, according to this view, the present-day Jews are from the tribe of Judah, are under a divine curse, and are not to be identified with Israel at all. Furthermore, the Anglo-Saxon peoples, including the British (i.e., Ephraim) and Americans (i.e., Manasseh) are the inheritors of the covenants and promises of the Old Testament.

In addition to some misunderstood scriptural arguments based on the birthright of Joseph (Gen. 49:26) and the promises to his sons Ephraim and Manasseh (48:20), British-Israelism maintains that the lost tribes left landmarks on their trek across Europe. Thus, the Dan and Danube Rivers, as well as the city of Danzig and country of Denmark are clear indications to them of the tribe of Dan! The term "Saxons" is supposedly a contraction of "Isaac's Sons," while the term "British" is actually derived from two Hebrew words for "covenant" and "man"! These linguistic arguments have been rejected by every reputable Hebrew scholar as absolutely groundless.

The original proponents of British-Israelism were evangelical and orthodox in the rest of their theology, and some still exist today, not as a separate denomination, but as a small movement which is found in many different churches. What should cause real concern, however, is the way in which this view has been adopted into the teachings of two groups which are clearly out of line with the main tenets of biblical Christianity. The first of these is known as the Worldwide Church of God, founded by the late Herbert W. Armstrong.

Armstrong made British-Israelism a vital part of his doctrinal system, which also denies the deity of the Holy Spirit and the reality of everlasting punishment. Armstrong's theology further imposes the Old Testament laws on the believer as a means of salvation.

Another group which has adopted British-Israelism is the "Identity" movement of white supremacy. A number of groups, affirming the satanic character of Zionism and the so-called worldwide Jewish conspiracy, have adopted British-Israelism to prove the superiority of the white race over Jews, Asiatics, and Negroes. These groups have often led demonstrations against the supposed Jewish control of money and the media, as well as engaging in violent actions against so-called Jewish "enemies."

WHAT IS THE SCRIPTURAL HISTORY OF THE 10 LOST TRIBES?

A detailed refutation of the many explanations of the history of Israel's northern tribes is impossible within the scope of this chapter. The great Hebrew-Christian scholar, David Baron, in his work *The History of the Ten "Lost" Tribes* has provided the most detailed and accurate answer to the question.[1] The following is a summary of his main points with a few additional observations of the author.

The fallacy inherent in all of the theories about the lost tribes is simply this: they were never lost, but continued as part of the main body of the Jewish people. To illustrate the truthfulness of this statement, consider the following five points:

1. At the time of the disruption of the United Kingdom in 930 BC, faithful Israelites from all the northern tribes joined their brethren in the south and continued their identity as part of the kingdom of Judah. Two books in Scripture that are strangely ignored by British-Israelites are 1 and 2 Chronicles. These books make it clear that the tribes in the north continued their existence as part of Judah after 930 BC. Consider 2 Chronicles 11:14, 16: "For the Levites left their suburban lands and their possession, and came to Judah and Jerusalem; for Jeroboam and his sons had cast them off from executing the priest's office unto the LORD. And after them, out of all the tribes of Israel, such as set their hearts to seek the LORD God of Israel came to Jerusalem, to sacrifice unto the LORD God of their fathers." These verses provide irrefutable proof that many godly individuals out of "all the tribes of Israel" rejected Jeroboam's idolatry and joined the southern kingdom. During the reign of Asa, others followed from Ephraim and Manasseh (15:9). Thus, it is evident that the kingdom of Judah absorbed many from the northern kingdom through the years.

2. Although it is often assumed that all of the northern kingdom went into the Assyrian captivity, Scripture teaches that Israelites continued to live there after the captivity of 721 BC. Again, Chronicles helps us in this regard. At Hezekiah's invitation, many from the north settled in Judah after the destruction of the northern kingdom (2 Chr. 30). Even later, in 622 BC, more godly Israelites came to Jerusalem to help repair the Temple (34:9), and later to celebrate the Passover (35:17–18). If the northern tribes had become lost, how could these representatives have joined in worship in Jerusalem 100 years after the Assyrian destruction? A reading of the chronicler's account forces one to the conclusion that not all of the northern tribes went into captivity in 721 BC.

Archaeology has confirmed this fact which is so clearly taught in Chronicles. Excavations have revealed that the population of Judah rapidly increased after the fall of the northern kingdom as a result of the many refugees mentioned in 2 Chronicles 11:14–16. Furthermore, archaeologists have uncovered the annals of the Assyrian Sargon, in which he tells that he carried away only 27,290 people and 50 chariots (*Biblical Archaeologist*, VI, 1943, p. 58). Since estimates of the population of the northern kingdom at that time range from 400,000 to 500,000, clearly less than one-twentieth of the population was deported, primarily the leaders from the area around Samaria. The 10 tribes, therefore, were never lost because they were never deported! Their kingdom was destroyed and ceased to exist, but most of them stayed, with some around Samaria intermingling with new immigrants to form the Samaritans (2 Ki. 17:24–41).

3. When the Jews returned from their Babylonian captivity in 536 BC and the following years, the chronicler viewed the restored community as the remnant of all Israel, both north and south, and not just the tribe of Judah: "Now the first inhabitants who dwelt in their possessions in their cities were the Israelites, the priests, Levites, and the Nethinim. And in Jerusalem dwelt of the children of Judah, and of the children of Benjamin, and of the children of Ephraim, and Manasseh" (1 Chr. 9:2–3). According to these verses, we should look to find Ephraim and Manasseh, not in England and America, but in Jerusalem following the return from Babylon.

Furthermore, the people at that time viewed themselves as part of all Israel, for they offered "twelve he-goats, according to the number of the tribes of Israel" (Ezra 6: 17). Although British-Israelism confidently asserts that Judah and Israel are always separate and distinct, a concordance shows that in the book of Ezra the restored community is called "Jews" only eight times and "Israel" 50 times. The writer evidently viewed the terms as interchangeable, both applying to the same people after the captivity.

4. The New Testament clearly indicates that there were individuals in the first century who still maintained their tribal identities—some of whom were members of those supposedly lost tribes. Consider, for example, the aged Anna who beheld the baby Jesus in the Temple. Luke 2:36 states that she was of the "tribe of Asher."

When Paul spoke of his Jewish brethren, he spoke of a common promise and a common hope: "Unto which promise our twelve tribes, earnestly serving God day and night, hope to come" (Acts 26:7). James addressed his epistle "to the twelve tribes which are scattered abroad" (Jas. 1:1). He made no distinction between Judah and 10 tribes. All Jews were part of a common body, the only difference being that some were in the land of Israel and some in the Diaspora. Evidently, members of all the tribes existed both inside and outside the Promised Land.

The New Testament uses the term *Jew* 174 times and the term *Israel*

75 times, clearly applying them to the same body of people. It is also striking that the apostle Paul referred to himself as both a "Jew" (Acts 22:3) and an "Israelite" (Rom. 11:1), and there is never a time when he distinguishes between Jews and Israel, as modern British-Israelism does. If the so-called lost tribes indeed resurfaced as the British people, and if Jeremiah eventually traveled to Britain to establish David's throne there, one would expect some trace of these matters to be mentioned in the New Testament. The silence of the New Testament writers in this regard, however, is deafening. The New Testament refers to only one group of people who descended from Jacob: "Who are Israelites; to whom pertaineth the adoption, and the glory, and the covenants, and the giving of the law, and the service of God, and the promises; whose are the fathers, and of whom, as concerning the flesh, Christ came, who is over all, God blessed forever. Amen" (Rom. 9:4–5).

5. Biblical prophecy concerning the end-times also indicates continuing tribal distinctions. Although Jews today do not know from which tribe they are descended (with the possible exception of the Levites), Scripture affirms that God knows. Such passages as Revelation 7:4–8 and Ezekiel 48 declare that representatives of restored Israel will be present in the Tribulation and also in the Millennial Kingdom. More complete consideration of these and other prophetic passages about the tribes will be given in the next chapter.

SUMMARY

To summarize, it can be said, on the basis of Scripture, history, and archaeology, that there is no such thing as the 10 lost tribes. What was lost was the separate existence of the kingdom of Israel in the north. The tribes, however, continued to exist in the body of the southern kingdom with the terms "Jews" and "Israel" applied to all of the covenant people after the captivity.

Furthermore, any claim that some ethnic group descended from the 10 tribes rests on shaky biblical and historical foundations. British-Israelism, in addition to distorting the Scriptures through its preconceived bias, fosters national pride and is helping to fuel the white supremacist, anti-Semitic groups that are spreading their poisonous propaganda today. Satan's attempts to destroy the Jewish people have taken various forms in history, from the days of Antiochus Epiphanes to the murderous plan of Hitler. Now the evil one is promoting the lie that the Jews are not truly the Jews, thus robbing Israel of its promises and covenants and transferring them to the Anglo-Saxon race!

Let us continue to be confident in the plain promises of Scripture and not be led astray by the misinterpretations and fanciful imaginings of man!

CHAPTER TWELVE

The Tribes of Israel in the End-Times

Jacob's deathbed blessings on his 12 sons recorded in Genesis 49 were also prophecies of the future characteristics of the tribes that came from the 12 sons. All of these prophecies have been fulfilled in the subsequent scriptural history of the tribes. Other Scriptures, however, indicate that the tribes will figure in a significant way in yet-to-be-fulfilled prophecies during the end-times. This chapter will explore some of the false and true concepts concerning the role of the tribes of Israel in fulfilled biblical prophecy.

UNSCRIPTURAL TEACHING

There are two views giving false interpretations to the future of the tribes of Israel. The first states that there is no separate future prophesied for the tribes apart from their involvement with the church. This view is usually associated with Amillennialism, which teaches that all the covenant promises of blessing to Israel have their fulfillment in the present-day church, which is now identified as spiritual Israel. The Millennial Kingdom, therefore, is presently being experienced, and all believers, Jewish or Gentile, spiritually are the tribes of the new Israel.

The problem with this view is its principle of spiritualized rather than literal interpretation. According to this principle, prophetic references to Israel, Zion, Jerusalem, etc. are interpreted as referring to God's people in this age (i.e., the church). This was not the method employed, however, by the New Testament writers and especially by the apostle

Paul in Romans 11. In that crucial chapter, Paul, the Jewish believer, described the present condition of unbelieving Israel and the future condition of believing Israel (vv. 25–27). Any interpretation that regards the initial references to Israel in Romans 11:1–24 as the Jewish people and the later references to Israel as the church is not only inconsistent with the context of the chapter but also empties plain language of any sensible meaning. Yes, according to both the Old and New Testaments, the tribes of Israel do have a future.

The second false interpretation views the future of the tribes, particularly the 10 northern tribes, as being associated with England and America. This view, known as British-Israelism, was discussed in the previous chapter and shown to be historically, linguistically, and scripturally in error. Much emphasis is placed by British-Israelites on the prophecy of Jacob regarding Ephraim and Manasseh in Genesis 48:17-22. There Jacob prophesied concerning Ephraim: "His seed shall become a multitude of nations" (v. 19). British-Israelism claims that the many nations in the British Commonwealth are the fulfillment of this prophecy. Apart from the fact that Britain's commonwealth has all but disappeared, this view neglects the scriptural meaning of "nations." The term *goyim*, generally referring to the Gentile nations, is also used for the tribes or families of the Jewish people! Here is a literal translation of the key Scripture: "And He said unto me, Son of Man, I send thee to the children of Israel, to nations [the plural *goyim* in Hebrew] that are rebellious, which have rebelled against Me" (Ezek. 2:3). The *Theological Wordbook of the Old Testament* (p. 154) states, "In this general ethnic sense the term *goy* may even be used of Abraham's seed"[1] (cf. Gen. 12:2; 17:20; 21:18; Ex. 33:13; Dt. 4:6–7; Josh. 3:17; 5:8). The fulfillment of this prophecy to Ephraim was found in the large population and influence of that tribe in subsequent years, not in the Anglo Saxon peoples—a people of Japhetic, not Semitic, ancestry.

SCRIPTURAL TEACHING

The New Testament contains some fascinating truths about the future of Israel's tribes. In fact, prophecies of the tribes are associated with the four major events of biblical eschatology—the Tribulation, the Second Coming, the Millennial reign, and the new heavens and Earth.

THE TRIBULATION

The major section of the book of The Revelation (chapters 4 through 19) describes events during a seven-year period commonly referred to as the Tribulation period. Chapter 7 is an inset between the sixth and seventh seal judgments (cf. Rev. 6:12–17 and 8:1). In that chapter, two large groups of people appear who represent those saved during that awful period known in the Old Testament as "the time of Jacob's trouble" (Jer. 30:7). The first group is described in Revelation 7:4–8:

> *And I heard the number of them which were sealed; and there were sealed an hundred and forty and four thousand of all the tribes of the children of Israel. Of the tribe of Judah were sealed twelve thousand. Of the tribe of Reuben were sealed twelve thousand. Of the tribe of Gad were sealed twelve thousand. Of the tribe of Asher were sealed twelve thousand. Of the tribe of Naphtali were sealed twelve thousand. Of the tribe of Manasseh were sealed twelve thousand. Of the tribe of Simeon were sealed twelve thousand. Of the tribe of Levi were sealed twelve thousand. Of the tribe of Issachar were sealed twelve thousand. Of the tribe of Zebulun were sealed twelve thousand. Of the tribe of Joseph were sealed twelve thousand. Of the tribe of Benjamin were sealed twelve thousand.*

This group of 144,000 is clearly described as "of all the tribes of the children of Israel" (Rev. 7:4). There are some, however, who want to reject the obvious meaning of Scripture and apply this passage to their own religious cult (e.g., the Watchtower Society). The apostle John went to much effort, however, to convey that this group is entirely Jewish by mentioning that 12,000 came from each of the 12 tribes and even giving the tribal names! Furthermore, John contrasts this group with an innumerable non-Jewish group in Revelation 7:9–17, who are described as being "of all nations, and kindreds, and peoples, and tongues" (v. 9). This should clearly prove the Jewish nature of the 144,000 and forever silence those who want to identify them as the church or some other religious group.

These sealed Jews are those who come to faith in Jesus as Messiah during the Tribulation period. They are further described as "first fruits unto God and to the Lamb" (14:4), indicating that they compose the first stage of a final harvest of Jewish souls to be gathered later at the Lord's coming in glory. Some interpreters have taught that these Jews will become evangelists to all the world during this dark hour. Although this may be true, we must be careful to emphasize only what the passage teaches (i.e., that a large body of Jews will be saved and protected from the Tribulation judgments). These comprise the "remnant" of Jews "who keep the commandments of God, and have the testimony of Jesus Christ" (12:17).

A comparison of this passage with the other tribal listings in Scripture reveals the absence of Ephraim and Dan. In an earlier chapter, it was seen that the tribe of Dan was overrun by idolatry from the days of the judges. Interestingly, Jeroboam's idols were placed in the tribes of Dan and Ephraim (i.e., Bethel, 1Ki. 12:29). Thus, in the Revelation 7 listing, Dan was replaced by Levi (v. 7) and Ephraim was replaced by his father Joseph (v. 8), while his brother Manasseh was included to complete the 12 (v. 6).

Many have asked, If Jews do not presently know their tribal membership, how can this prophecy be fulfilled? The answer, simply put, is: Human inability to comprehend such matters does not limit God's ability to know and sort out the details. The sealing will be done by angels who will perform His bidding, regardless of the lack of human knowledge in the matter.

THE SECOND COMING

The theme verse of The Revelation describes our Lord's advent with these words: "Behold, he cometh with clouds, and every eye shall see him, and they also who pierced him; and all kindreds of the earth shall wail because of him. Even so, Amen"(1:7). The fulfillment of this announcement does not actually occur until Revelation 19:11–16, which takes place after the Tribulation period. Most commentators explain this verse as describing the universal repentance of all the ethnic tribes of mankind at the Second Advent. These interpreters, however, have neglected to view the verse in its Old Testament context.

It is evident that Revelation 1:7 clearly refers to Zechariah 12:10: "And I will pour upon the house of David, and upon the inhabitants of Jerusalem, the Spirit of grace and of supplications; and they shall look upon me whom they have pierced, and they shall mourn for him, as one mourneth for his only son, and shall be in bitterness for him, as one that is in bitterness for his firstborn." In that context, those who look upon the "pierced" One are the inhabitants of Jerusalem and Judah (i.e., Jews). The mourners in Zechariah 12:11ff., are Jewish inhabitants of the land of Israel. This mourning is an indication of the penitential remorse to be experienced by Israel at its national conversion prophesied so often in both the Old and New Testaments (e.g., Hos. 3:5; Rom. 11:25–27).

The word *kindreds* in Revelation 1:7 is the Greek word *phyle*, translated "tribe" in Revelation 5:5 ("tribe of Judah") and in Revelation 7:4–8 ("tribes of the children of Israel"). Therefore, Revelation 1:7 is referring, not to a general mourning of mankind at the Second Coming, but to a mourning of repentance by Israel's tribes when they recognize their suffering Messiah. A parallel thought was expressed by the Lord Jesus in Matthew 24:30: "And then shall appear the sign of the Son of man in heaven; and then shall all the tribes of the earth mourn, and they shall see the Son of man coming in the clouds of heaven with power and great glory." Perhaps the Servant Song of Isaiah 53 will be the words used to express Israel's penitential cry. In that crucial chapter, Israel describes its suffering Messiah and its response to Him with these words:

> *Surely he hath borne our griefs, and carried our sorrows; yet we did esteem him stricken, smitten of God, and afflicted. But he was wounded for our transgressions, he was bruised for our iniquities; the chastisement for our peace was upon him, and with his stripes we are healed. All we like sheep have gone astray; we have turned every one to his own way, and the LORD hath laid on him the iniquity of us all* (Isa. 53:4-6).

In that day, the tribes of Israel will repentantly confess that the One they rejected was the One who actually came to suffer as an "offering" for their sin (v. 10).

THE MILLENNIAL REIGN

Following His Second Coming to Earth, the Messiah will reign over a restored Israel and a renewed Earth for a thousand years (Zech. 14:9; Isa.11:1–11; Rev. 20:1–6). During that Kingdom period, the tribes of

Israel again will play a prominent role. This was stated unequivocally by the Messiah Himself in Matthew 19:28: "And Jesus said unto them, Verily I say unto you that ye who have followed me, in the regeneration, when the Son of man shall sit on the throne of his glory, ye also shall sit upon twelve thrones, judging the twelve tribes of Israel." Peter wondered what reward he and his comrades would receive because they had forsaken all in this life to follow Jesus. He told them the physical reward would not come in this life but in the life to come, when the apostles would participate in the Millennial government.

Jesus referred to this time as the "regeneration" (Mt. 19:28), a word used only twice in the New Testament. In Titus 3:5 it refers to the regeneration of the individual soul; in Matthew 19:28 it refers to the regeneration of the earth during the Kingdom. Evidently, restored Israel, represented by the 12 tribes, will be governed by the 12 apostles as vice-regents to the King of kings in the Millennial administration. The eschatological concept of believers judging in the sense of governing also appears in Daniel 7:22; Luke 22:30; 1 Corinthians 6:2, and Revelation 20:4. The exact details of the governmental administration in the Millennium are not revealed in Scripture, but we can rest assured that the reign will be marked by justice, equity, and righteousness (cf. Isa. 11:3–5).

One other passage provides information on the role of the tribes during the Millennium. Ezekiel, chapters 40—48, one of the most fascinating and difficult passages in the Scriptures, describe the Millennial Temple, the regulations regarding its sacrifices and priestly duties and the appointment of the land to the various tribes.

The rabbis of the Talmud (Menachem 45a) remarked that only the prophet Elijah, who will herald the ultimate redemption, will be able to explain these chapters fully, No attempt will be made here to clarify all the details of this section of God's Word, but particular note should be taken of Ezekiel 48, where we find a description of the boundaries of the Millennial tribal divisions, which differ considerably from the original boundaries described in Joshua 13—19. A consideration of the map will help to illuminate the following details. The entire territory west of the Jordan River is to be divided into 12 parallel portions running east to west. The northern boundary is in the modern country of Lebanon. The southern boundary is roughly the same as Israel's present boundary with Egypt. Each tribe will receive an equal share in the following order from north to south: Dan, Asher, Naphtali, Manasseh, Ephraim, Reuben, Judah, Benjamin, Simeon, Issachar, Zebulun, Gad. Between the territories of Judah and Benjamin will be situated the "holy oblation" (Ezek. 48:10), comprising the Temple area and the domains of the priests, Levites and the "prince."

It is noteworthy that the tribes descended from the handmaids, Bilhah and Zilpah, are placed at the extreme ends, farthest from the sanctuary. It should also be noted that the tribe of Dan, although not included in the 144,000 Jews sealed during the Tribulation, will have its own portion in the Millennial Kingdom. Evidently this period, referred to by Peter as "the times of restitution of all things" (Acts 3:21), will witness the restoration of Dan's tribal inheritance as well.

Whatever be the precise interpretation of all these details, this much is clear: the presence of the glory of the Lord will be hallowed in the land. Jerusalem will even experience a name change: "The name of the city from that day shall be, The LORD is there" (Ezek. 48:35). The One whom Ezekiel had sadly witnessed departing in chapters 9—11 will gloriously return to His forsaken Temple (see Ezek. 43:1–5). Moreover, the tribes of Israel, long scattered in the lands of exile, will be regathered, restored, regenerated and ruled over by their Messiah King, the Lord Jesus Christ.

THE NEW HEAVENS AND EARTH

The final reference to the tribes of Israel in the Bible is in connection with John's vision of "a new heaven and a new earth" (Rev. 21:1). In Revelation 21:10, John also sees "that great city, the holy Jerusalem, descending out of heaven from God." That indescribably beautiful city is to be adorned with "twelve gates, and at the gates twelve angels, and names written on the gates, which are the names of the twelve tribes of the children of Israel" (v. 12). These gates are balanced by the 12 foundations of the wall which bear the names of the 12 apostles (v. 14).

Although this reference does not describe a separate role for the 12 tribes in that day, it does speak of the fact that throughout eternity the Old Testament people of God (i.e., the tribes) and the New Testament people of God (i.e., the apostles) will bask together in the light of the glory of God and of His Lamb (v. 23).

Thus, that which was planted in Genesis, the book of creation, finds its fruition in Revelation, the book of consummation. The sons who originally gathered around their aged father's deathbed scarcely realized that their descendants would play such a crucial role in the development of God's redemptive plan. For believers, a consideration of the overarching unity of this wide-ranging plan should cause us to rejoice in the words of the apostle Paul: "Oh, the depth of the riches both of the wisdom and knowledge of God! How unsearchable are his judgments, and his ways past finding out!" (Rom 11:33).

NOTES

CHAPTER 3: SIMEON AND LEVI

[1] George Lawson, *Lectures on the History of Joseph* (1807).
[2] Leon Wood, *A Survey of Israel's History* (Zondervan, 1970).

CHAPTER 5: ZEBULUN AND ISSACHAR

[1] Ephraim Avigdov Speiser, *The Anchor Bible: Genesis* (1964).
[2] Adam Clarke, *Commentary on the Bible* (1831).

CHAPTER 8: JOSEPH

[1] George Bush, *Questions and Notes Critical and Practical, Upon the Book of Genesis* (1831).

CHAPTER 9: BENJAMIN

[1] Matthew Henry, *Concise Commentary on the Whole Bible: Genesis* (1708-10).

CHAPTER 10: THESE ARE THE 12 TRIBES OF ISRAEL

[1] George Bush, *Questions and Notes Critical and Practical, Upon the Book of Exodus* (1871).

CHAPTER 11: WILL THE 10 LOST TRIBES EVER BE FOUND?

[1] David Baron, *The History of the Ten Lost Tribes* (1915).

CHAPTER 12: THE TRIBES OF ISRAEL IN THE END-TIMES

[1] R. Laird Harris, Gleason L. Archer, and Bruce K. Waltke, *Theological Wordbook of the Old Testament* (Moody Publishers, 1982).